A CRISIS IN CARE?
CHALLENGES TO SOCIAL WORK

FAMILY LIFE AND SOCIAL POLICY COURSE TEAM

Melanie Bayley, Editor

Ann Boomer, Secretary

David Boswell, Senior Lecturer in Sociology

Hilary Canneaux, Course Manager

John Clarke, Senior Lecturer in Social Policy

Allan Cochrane, Senior Lecturer in Urban Studies (Course Team Chair)

Juliette Cowan, Secretary

Rudi Dallos, Staff Tutor, Social Sciences

Harry Dodd, Print Production Controller

Peggotty Graham, Staff Tutor, Social Sciences

Pauline Harris, Staff Tutor, Social Sciences; Open University Tutor

Tom Hunter, Editor

Bernie Lake, Secretary

Mary Langan, Lecturer in Social Policy

Jack Leathem, Producer, BBC/OUPC

Vic Lockwood, Senior Producer, BBC/OUPC

Eugene McLaughlin, Lecturer in Criminology and Social Policy

Ione Mako, Production Assistant, BBC/OUPC

Dorothy Miell, Lecturer in Psychology

John Muncie, Senior Lecturer in Criminology and Social Policy

Roger Sapsford, Senior Lecturer in Research Methods

Esther Saraga, Staff Tutor, Social Sciences

Jane Sheppard, Designer

Richard Skellington, Project Officer, Social Sciences

Paul Smith, Social Sciences Liaison Librarian

Margaret Wetherell, Senior Lecturer in Psychology

Fiona Williams, Senior Lecturer in the School of Health, Welfare and Community Education

Michael Wilson, Senior Lecturer in Research Methods

David Wilson, Editor

Consultant authors

John Baldock, Senior Lecturer in Social Policy, University of Kent

Elizabeth Barrett, Training Officer, Ford Motor Company Ltd., Basildon, Essex

Rosaleen Croghan, Research Assistant; Open University Tutor

Sally Foreman, Research Psychologist; Open University Tutor

Norman Ginsburg, Principal Lecturer in Social Policy, South Bank University, London

Hilary Land, Professor of Social Policy, Royal Holloway and Bedford New College, University of London

Lynne Segal, Principal Lecturer, School of Psychology, Middlesex University

George Taylor, Senior Lecturer in Social Work, De Montfort University, Leicester

External assessors

Hilary Graham, Professor of Applied Social Studies, University of Warwick (Course Assessor)

Kum Kum Bhavnani, Lecturer in Applied Social Studies, University of Bradford

Caroline McKinlay, Publications Officer, Women's Aid Federation, England

Raymond Taylor, Prinicpal Training Officer in Social Work, Central Regional Council, Stirling

Tutor panel

Rosemary Collins, Open University Tutor

Helen Cowie, Senior Lecturer in Social Studies, Bretton Hall, University of Leeds; Open University Tutor.

A CRISIS IN CARE? CHALLENGES TO SOCIAL WORK

EDITED BY
JOHN CLARKE

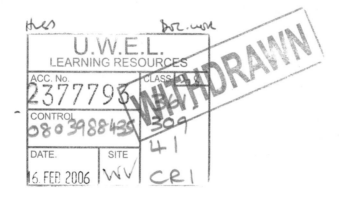
SAGE Publications

LONDON • NEWBURY PARK • NEW DELHI

PUBLISHED IN ASSOCIATION WITH

The Open University

The Open University, Walton Hall, Milton Keynes, MK7 6AA.

First published 1993. Reprinted 1994, 1995, 1997

SAGE Publications Ltd
6 Bonhill Street
London EC2A 4PU

SAGE Publications Inc
2455 Teller Road
Newbury Park, California 91320

SAGE Publications India Pvt Ltd
32, M-Block Market
Greater Kailash–1
New Delhi 110 048

British Library Cataloguing in Publication Data

Crisis in care? Challenges to social work.

John Clarke

ISBN 0–8039–8843–5

ISBN 0–8039–8844–3 Pbk

361.30941

Library of Congress catalog card number 92-051075

Edited, Designed and Typeset by the Open University.

Printed in the United Kingdom by Butler and Tanner Ltd, Frome and London.

This text forms part of an Open University Third Level Course, *D311 Family Life and Social Policy*. If you would like a copy of *Studying with the Open University*, please write to the Course Reservations and Sales Centre, PO Box 724, The Open University, Walton Hall, Milton Keynes, MK7 6ZS, United Kingdom.

CONTENTS

CHAPTER I
THE COMFORT OF STRANGERS: SOCIAL
WORK IN CONTEXT

CHAPTER 2
UNDERSTANDING PEOPLE: THE GROWTH OF
AN EXPERTISE

CHAPTER 5
CHALLENGES FROM THE MARGINS

CHAPTER 6
NEW DIRECTIONS IN SOCIAL WORK

PREFACE

This book is concerned with the changing fortunes of social work in Britain. It explores the nineteenth century origins of social work in a range of settings and considers the conditions underpinning its subsequent rise to become a 'fifth social service' in the British welfare state. The main focus of the book is the crisis of public, political and professional confidence which has come to dominate social work since the 1970s. The nature of this crisis is examined through a range of challenges to social work both from the political centre of British society and from its margins. Social work occupies a special position in the British welfare system as a point of intersection between social policy and the family. As such it is peculiarly exposed to changing views and arguments about the relationship between the public realm of policy and politics and the private sphere of individual and familial living.

This book is one of a series published by Sage which is concerned with the relationships between families and the development and practice of social policy. The other three books in the series are *Understanding the Family* (edited by John Muncie, Margaret Wetherell, Mary Langan, Rudi Dallos and Allan Cochrane), *Social Problems and the Family* (edited by Rudi Dallos and Eugene McLaughlin), and *Comparing Welfare States: Britain in International Context* (edited by Allan Cochrane and John Clarke). Each of the books in the series looks at the ways in which professional and state sponsored interventions help to shape the experience of family life in different contexts. Each also considers the ways in which particular notions of the family influence the development of social policy. We believe that only by bringing these debates together is it possible to understand key aspects of the welfare regimes being constructed in the 1990s.

This series of books was initially written as part of an Open University course (D311 *Family Life and Social Policy*), which is, as its title implies, principally concerned with the complex interrelationships between the family and the state. The family is frequently understood as a private arena within which individuals are essentially free to determine how they live their own lives. The state, on the other hand is often presented as the complete antithesis, at worst seeking to interfere in matters which should be left to private decision making, at best helping to provide a wider — public — context within which individuals and families may interact.

The course questions these dichotomies and explores the greater complexities of family life in the United Kingdom at the end of the twentieth century. It uses insights from psychology, social policy and sociology to develop its arguments, starting with a focus on the internal life of families, moving through a consideration of forms of social and professional intervention towards a comparative analysis of social policy in Europe and a consideration of possible futures. At the core of the course are concerns about the relationships between the public and private spheres, about the need to acknowledge and explore diversity in the lived experience of families and about the ways in which power and inequality work themselves out within and between families. These concerns are also central to all the books in this series.

The chapters of this book have been substantially informed by debates within the course team, drawing on ideas, evidence and method from a range of disciplines. In other words they are the products of a genuinely interdisciplinary process in which we have all learned from each other. Without these debates and regular discussion it would have been impossible to produce this book. In such a collaborative process it should be clear that important contributions have been made to all of the chapters by people who are not explicitly named as authors.

An Open University Course Team stretches far beyond the core of academics who write for it, to include consultants, tutor-testers and assessors who give invaluable advice, a course manager who somehow brings the pieces together, editors and designers who make it all look good, and secretaries who manage — against all the odds — to produce high quality manuscripts to deadlines which everybody else does their best to forget. The work of all of these people is reflected in this book as well as in other parts of the course. We thank them for it.

ACKNOWLEDGEMENTS

Grateful acknowledgement is made to the following sources for permission to reproduce material in this book:

TEXT

Chapter 4: Wood, N., 'Councils "should give up" social worker role', *The Times*, 3 January 1991, © Times Newspapers Ltd 1991; Department of Health (1991), *Child Abuse: a Study of Inquiry Reports 1980-1989*, reproduced with the permission of the Controller of Her Majesty's Stationery Office; Butler-Sloss, E. (1988), *Report of the Enquiry into Child Abuse in Cleveland 1987*, Cmd 412, reproduced with the permission of the Controller of Her Majesty's Stationery Office; Chapter 5: Smart, D. (1991), 'A chance for gay people', *Community Care*, 24 January 1991, Reed Business Publishing Ltd; Owusu-Bempah, J. (1990), 'Toeing the white line', *Community Care*, 1 November 1990, Reed Business Publishing Ltd; Morris, J. (1989), 'Women confronting disability', *Community Care*, 29 June 1989, Reed Business Publishing Ltd; Kelly, E. (1988), 'Talking about a revolution', *Spare Rib,* no. 193, August 1988.

TABLES

Tables 3.1 and 3.2: adapted from Hayes, P. et al. (1989), *Social Work In Crisis: a Study of Conditions in Six Local Authorities*, courtesy of NALGO.

PHOTOGRAPHS

Page 107: from *Community Care*; page 115: John Birdsall Photography; page 123: Copyright Jane Bown.

INTRODUCTION

JOHN CLARKE

This book is concerned with the changing fortunes of social work in Britain. The focus upon social work is a result of its special position in the field of family life and social policy. Social work developed as a form of intervention which explicitly claimed to provide the attention to individual and familial circumstances which were absent from the bureaucratic and insensitive large scale institutions of social welfare. Its practice has formed a distinctive link between the private realms of personal and family life and the public domain of social policy. Social work has provided a form of social intervention which has both 'personalized' social policy, linking the individual to the systems of social welfare, and extended the reach of the state into the intimate circumstances of domestic life. While not the only form of social welfare to combine the public and the private in this way, social work has acquired a distinctive public visibility concerning its involvement in family lives. By contrast, other forms of intervention have remained relatively invisible. Social work, then, has come to stand for a particular set of issues and conflicts about the relationship between the state and the family. Our concern in this book is to explore the distinctive features of this special position by examining the forces which have shaped the development of social work in Britain.

As other studies of the same subject have found, pinning down exactly what is meant by social work can prove to be a difficult and even frustrating task. Our starting point for this book is the view that such a search for the 'essence' of social work is doomed to failure. On the contrary, it is precisely the diverse and fragmentary nature of social work — its scattering across different sites and institutions, its relationships with different 'client groups' and its adoption of different approaches to theory and practice — that is the subject of our interest here. Trying to force this diversity into a single mould by discovering the 'real heart' of social work does an injustice to both its history and the present dilemmas and choices which confront social work and social workers.

Our approach here is somewhat different. We start from the position that from the very first attempts to formalize and systematize the practice of social work in the nineteenth century, social work itself has been characterized by diversity and fragmentation. In some ways, this multiple character of social work derives from the variety of institutional settings in and around which forms of social work were developed — the courts, hospitals, the Poor Law, and charitable initiatives. In others, it derives from the variety of approaches to the 'social work task' — arguments over the primary methods, theories and concerns which were supposed to govern the practice of social work. In still different ways, it derives from the multiple and competing objectives established as the aims of social work — arising from the diverse constituencies which have both directed and been served by social work.

One of the objectives of this book, then, is to chart some of the forces and pressures which have contributed to and sustained social work as a highly complex collection of contexts, personnel and practices. Such conditions mean that social work has constantly been a variety of different 'social works' — likely to separate out into its fragmentary components or to move in different directions in response to conflicting pressures and demands. These forces have themselves changed since the late nineteenth century, and the accounts presented in the chapters of this book attempt to register the shifting salience of different pressures on and expectations of social work.

Our second objective is to explore some of the ways in which attempts have been made to provide some coherence to social work — to create an apparent unity out of this diversity. At different times during social work's development, these efforts to create a unified profession have taken different routes — identifying particular elements which the diversity of sites and approaches to social work have in common. The book can, therefore, be read as a study of the tension between the forces which pull towards fragmentation and the attempts to provide some form of occupational coherence. Chapter 1 examines the emergence of social work on the margins of nineteenth century institutions, extending the scope of social care and control beyond the walls of the institutions into the community. It considers the significance of the growing involvement of the state in the organization of social work as an occupation and form of welfare provision. Chapter 2 explores the dependence of social work on the emergent science of psychology which promised a coherent knowledge-base — the means of 'understanding people' — to underpin the claims and practice of social work as a form of social intervention.

Chapter 3 considers the expanding role of social work as a form of state intervention through the emergence of 'generic' social work and its distinctive institutional location (social service departments) at the end of the 1960s. This high point of professional and political optimism involved a combination of attempts to provide social work with both a professional and an organizational coherence in an effort to overcome the multiplicity of 'social works' which existed in post-war Britain.

Chapters 4 and 5 explore social work's 'fall from grace' during the 1970s and 1980s under the intensification of competing and conflicting pressures on state social work. Chapter 4 looks at the changing evaluations and expectations of social work which emerged from the central state — both from governments and judicial inquiries — marking the development of a new series of demands on the organization and practice of social work in the 1990s. Chapter 5, by contrast, considers the emergence of challenges to social work theory and practice in the name of users and potential users of its services — directed at social work's exercise of power and discretion over users' concerns. The conclusion of the book explores the implications of these shifting demands and pressures for the future of social work in Britain.

That is an outline of the book. But we must also give some attention to one thing which the book is not about. We have used the word 'profession' in relation to social work both in this introduction and in the subsequent chapters and this raises the prospect of considerable difficulties over whether social work can be properly classified as a profession. There is a large and complex sociological literature devoted to the study of professions which offers a variety of approaches to the classification of professions, predominantly concerned with whether they posses a number of definable 'traits' (e.g., whether they regulate entry, possess a clearly defined body of knowledge or expertise). The application of such approaches to social work has itself produced a diversity of responses, mostly identifying the limited nature of social work's professionalism — expressed in such terms as 'quasi-profession', 'semi-profession' or 'professional bureaucracy'. We must confess that we are not particularly concerned with pursuing the discussion of whether social work can or cannot be properly classified as a profession. Our interest lies in the claims which social work has made, at different points in its development, to be viewed and treated *as if it was* a profession. We are interested in the conditions for such claims, the resources which are called upon in making them and the occupational and social consequences of such claims being made. That is to say, we are interested in professionalism to the extent that it can be viewed as one of the strategies used to promote a unity or coherence for social work in the face of conflicting pressures. As a consequence, we shall not be posing, much less answering, the question of whether social work is *really* a profession.

Our aim is that by focusing on the dynamics of social work's development, we can highlight the shifting networks of conflicting demands and expectations which have shaped social work. Alongside these we consider the varying strategies which have been used to promote the unification of social work — to fill the 'empty centre' which is the effect of the diverse and fragmented bases of social work in Britain. In that context, professionalism is one, but only one, of the strategies which have been pursued in the quest for coherence.

CHAPTER 1
THE COMFORT OF STRANGERS:
SOCIAL WORK IN CONTEXT

JOHN CLARKE

In the late twentieth century, it is taken for granted that some of our needs for care and personal support will be met by strangers — people whose job of work it is to respond to and deal with intimate aspects of our lives and personalities. Our society contains a range of 'helping professions' — social workers, welfare officers, counsellors and therapists of various kinds. Yet this pattern of personal needs being met by paid professionals is a relatively recent development. Before the nineteenth century, individuals requiring care and support, where their personal or social circumstances made them vulnerable, might have found assistance from three sources. They might have been assisted and cared for by and within their family networks or local communities, although such care depended on the willingness and capacity of the community to offer such support. They might have sought assistance from local Poor Law agencies if they were faced by poverty or destitution and, in the most desperate circumstances, they might have been taken into the workhouses. They might also have been taken in by one of the charitable institutions (mostly religious foundations) whose vocation it was to tend orphans, the elderly, the sick or those with disabilities. Such patterns of care were, of course, highly uneven and highly localized (see, e.g., Henriques, 1979 and Murphy, 1992). By the middle of the nineteenth century these patterns of support were seen as being no longer adequate to the task of meeting social needs.

The combination of two processes — industrialization (the growth of the factory system of production) and urbanization (the movement of people from the country to the towns in search of employment) — reshaped patterns of social needs. It also changed the conditions under which such needs might be met. Industrialization created new demands for labour and redefined the categories of people who could be seen as suitable labourers — marginalizing many who were identified as 'unfit' to staff the new factories. Alongside this redefinition of useful employment there emerged the problems of low waged employment, seasonal and cyclical unemployment and the resultant poverty of those who were dependent on the wage to live. The rapid expansion of the towns created new problems of housing, unsanitary living conditions and ill health. These new urban conditions also seemed to represent the collapse of 'community' and the patterns of mutual interdependence and support which previous generations had found in their communities.

While the nineteenth century vision of these rural communities was highly romanticized, the ideal nonetheless fed a genuine social fear about the effects of loss of community and the prospect of social dislocation in the towns (Steadman-Jones, 1971). This fear manifested itself in a variety of middle-class concerns about the potential for misery, need, disorder and disruption which seemed to be built into the social fabric of the rapidly expanding towns and cities. It led to efforts to document poverty, sickness, crime and the other social consequences of the 'perishing classes' — those on the margins of the new urban-industrialized centres (Pearson, 1975, Chapter 6). What emerged from such documents of nineteenth century research, journalism and fiction was a stream of images of need arising from both personal and social circumstances for which the existing arrangements for care, control and support were hopelessly inadequate. The capacities of traditional charitable institutions were outrun by the growing pressures of need and the institutions themselves were inefficient, corrupt or corruptible (by those who wanted to exploit charity rather than work). At the same time, the dislocation of community meant both the failure of support and the absence of social leadership — a growing geographical and social gulf between classes where (in the image of the rural community at least) they had been bonded together by geographical proximity and ties of mutual obligation and responsibility (Steadman-Jones, 1971). The late nineteenth century saw the creation of responses to social problems which formed the structure that still dominates the provision of personal care in late twentieth century Britain.

I   CLASSIFIED RESULTS

The first element of nineteenth century reform was to reconstruct the institutions to a greater level of integration with the demands of an urban-industrial social order. The demands of this new order were complex. At their heart was the creation and maintenance of a population 'fit to work' in the new systems of production. Alongside this was a concern to strengthen an appropriate system of social values centring around thrift, sobriety, self-discipline and family life. Against this 'new order', it was apparent that a range of people and behaviour patterns were 'disorderly': social problems which threatened the search for a stabilized and harmonious society. The institutions of care and control themselves needed to be reformed, and new institutions created, to play a role in minimizing the damage which social problem groups might cause to this new order. Two things are striking about this process of reconstruction: the rapid multiplication of *types* of institution and the increasing significance of scientific principles of classifying the population into distinct categories to fit the different types of institutions. By the end of the nineteenth century, both the state and voluntary organizations had constructed a complex array of institutions designed to house, care for or reform a variety of people who were seen as constituting different types of social problem: the workhouse, the prison, the asylum, the school, borstals and reformatories, hospitals, and residential institutions for children. Each institution had its own particular character but all shared some common features. They all invoked the need to *segregate* the 'problem' — to subject it to an institutional regime separated from the rest of society. They all laid claim to a potential for *reform* — to remake the problem into a person capable, as the Prison Department put it, of 'leading a good and useful life'. And, in the service of reform, they all increasingly laid claim to a specialist or expert *'knowledge-base'* — a set of scientifically based under-standings of the problem and the principles of reform. These were intended to be *productive* institutions, taking in flawed human material, working on it in accordance with scientific principles and through such work creating a product useful to society. Given the combination of these principles with the belief that performing useful labour was the principal agency of 'reform' (whether such labour was men quarrying at Dartmoor prison or children picking fruit in rural residential institutions), some commentators have suggested that it was the factory that provided the model for the nineteenth century burst of institutional building enthusi-asm (Melossi and Pavarini, 1981).

Hand in hand with the reconstruction and development of institutions went an enormous growth of the scientific classification and examination of the human population. Based on medical, biological and subsequently psychological sciences, there was a feverish endeavour to divide, sub-divide, analyse and categorize different groups within the population. The full flowering of this endeavour is too extensive for us to catalogue here but we can indicate some of the major classificatory principles. One was the principle of *age* — the identification and conceptualization of childhood and the establishment of the principles of 'normal childhood development'; followed by the increasingly significant demarcation of adolescence as a distinct phase of life to be separated from both childhood and adulthood; and finally, the discovery and segregation of old age as a further distinct stage characterized by dependency. A second was the principle of *'able-bodiedness'* — against which were developed the categories of physical and mental impairment which were seen to disqual-ify their possessor from participating normally in economic, social and political life. A third was the classification of *gender* — identifying the traits and characteristics that made men and women different (and com-plementary). A fourth was the discovery of 'normal' and 'abnormal' *sexu-alities* — the classification of homosexuality in particular as a deviant condition — allied to the identification of normal sexual 'drives' (for men, at least) and practices (Mort, 1987). Other 'deviant' conditions were also the focus of much classificatory attention — criminals, delinquents, the insane and so on. Each of these conditions developed its own specialist knowledge and expert practitioners, and each its own set of rules which helped to identify the difference between the 'normal' (independent and autonomous adults) and the 'abnormal' or 'deviant' minority requiring special attention. These knowledges organized the regimes of the insti-tutions, governing how individuals were to be treated, how their 'progress' was to be measured and what principles should control the reform of the deviant. The populations of these institutions (whether children in the schoolroom or convicts in the prison) also provided the captive material for further research to fuel the growth of these human sciences.

There is one further classificatory principle to which it is worth drawing attention, and that is the classification of *race*. The same sciences led the way in this domain — identifying racial types by bodily characteristics, mental capacities and emotional traits. Here, too, there were hierarchies of 'development', with white Anglo-Saxons as the highest stage of development and other 'races' positioned by their greater or lesser approximation to this desirable norm or by their greater or lesser degree of progress on the evolutionary scale. Although there was no single institutional focus for this knowledge, its effects were felt across the entire fabric of British society: here, justifying repression of the Irish or the construction of the Aliens Act to prevent the importation of foreign subversion; there, embodied in the missionary and colonial cultures which spread Christianity and the British way of life around the globe. It also manifested itself in a variety of initiatives taken during the late nineteenth and early twentieth centuries to improve the 'fitness' of the British race itself, from the introduction of school meals to concerns about eligibility to breed which bore particularly on those identified as physically or mentally impaired and thus being poor 'breeding stock'.

Some of the issues concerned with this proliferation of knowledge about people are pursued in Chapter 2. For the moment, though, we want to consider the other aspect of the reorganization of social care during the nineteenth century: the growing concern with 'care in the community' and how it intersected with this reconstruction of the institutions.

2   BEYOND THE WALLS

The concern about the collapse of community and the growing social gulf between the classes in urban settings provided the basis for a range of voluntary initiatives aimed at bridging this gap. The motivation for these initiatives derived from a complex mixture of compassion and fear. Widespread concern about poverty, ill health and poor housing evoked compassion for the 'victims' of these circumstances and inspired charitable efforts to help those in need. But such compassion was mingled with mistrust and fear. Fear centred on the potentially destructive effects of such social problems — their potential for causing violence, unrest or 'contamination' through both the spread of diseases and, more metaphorically, spreading inflammatory ideas about social inequality and social justice. At the same time, such mid-nineteenth century charitable initiatives were dogged by the anxiety that their efforts might be exploited by those unscrupulous enough to use charity to avoid the necessity of supporting themselves. The consequences of this complex of motives can be traced through the ways in which the urban middle classes sought to help those in need from the mid-nineteenth to the early twentieth centuries.

One aim of such initiatives was to establish personal contact through a voluntary visitor or helper who would provide practical assistance and advice. The personal contact was also seen as essential in providing those in need with an 'uplifting' moral example. These voluntary workers expressed a high degree of enormous self confidence in their ability to demonstrate how to behave as good and useful citizens. The range of issues which attracted such action is a wide one — helpers attached themselves to hospitals, prisons and courts; voluntary workers visited working-class homes to provide advice and assistance on health, home management and child care; other volunteers played a major part in helping the 'deserving' poor (those identified as in need through no fault of their own) with advice and limited forms of material assistance (though rarely money).

There are three significant features about these charitable origins of social care in the community. *First, they took place on the margins of the major institutions*, aiming either to assist those leaving them to adjust to the demands of life beyond the institution or to 'filter' those at risk of entering them by picking out those who could be helped in their natural habitat rather than becoming institutionalized. Thus, the police court missionaries (the forerunners of the Probation and After Care service) developed alongside the courts, offering assistance to those leaving prison and offering an alternative to imprisonment by promising to 'advise, assist and befriend' those discharged from the courts into their care (Bochel, 1976). Similarly, members of the Charity Organization Society worked alongside the Boards of Poor Law Guardians to separate the deserving from the undeserving poor and to provide advice and assistance which might help the deserving cases to become independent, e.g. by providing widows with the equipment needed to take in washing or sewing (Steadman-Jones, 1971; Young and Ashton, 1956; Woodroofe, 1962).

Second, these voluntary activities were dominated by women. They provided a range of activities outside the home for middle-class women (given that paid employment was deemed inappropriate for them) and were often focused on what were identified as 'women's issues' — concerns about home management, health, and child care. Such activities provided a major focus for the social and political concerns of middle-class women and the central involvement of women in charitable work offered the basis for a cross class set of alliances between middle- and working-class women centring on issues of family, home, health and child care (Walton, 1975, Part 1).

Third, many of these voluntary initiatives were overshadowed by the assumptions and norms of middle-class life. At the centre of these were assumptions about the distinction between the 'deserving' (or those worthy and capable of being 'rescued') and the 'undeserving' poor. Views of the poor in charitable activities rested on a belief in 'moral character' as the decisive feature in people's circumstances — no structural issues of power, employment or marginalization entered this moral calculus (Steadman-Jones, 1971). One result of this was the emphasis given to the mixture of 'practical' advice and personal example in the work of voluntary agencies. The aim was to make people become independent, rather than give material assistance, because material help, especially money, was seen to carry the risk of making its recipients more rather than less dependent.

3   IN SEARCH OF UNITY

These diverse fragments of social intervention form the origins of social work in Britain, and the diversification of types and places of providing social care and support was to continue throughout most of the twentieth century. In the midst of this diversity, four elements stand out as points of potential overlap or unification between the different branches of what became known as social work. The first concerns the search for a systematic approach to the practice of social work which increasingly came to focus on the method of casework with individuals and families (Woodroofe, 1962). The second concerns the search for a systematic approach to the understanding of both the problems and practice of social work which came to focus on the emergent psychological sciences. The third relates to where the different forms of social work were practised — at the intersection of the institutions and the community, such that workers operated both within and outside of institutions of care and control like prisons, hospitals and institutions for children. The fourth and final point of overlap lay in the growing intersection between these forms of social work and the state. Although most had their origins in voluntary and charitable initiatives, they developed during the twentieth century as part of state agencies, increasingly moving from volunteer to full time paid workers with a growing concern for training and qualifications.

The first two concerns are entangled in the development of a systematic approach to social work which attempted to transcend the diversity of places and forms of practice. By the 1940s, the casework method and its focus on the uniqueness of each individual/family configuration encountered by the social worker had come to dominate the theory and practice of social work in most of the different settings. The method required social workers to be attentive to the patterns of relationships and behaviours in the family groupings with whom they worked. It also helped to create the conditions in which psychology and related sciences were seen as representing the obvious theoretical support to the practice of social work. The psychological sciences more than any other approach held out the prospect of focusing on the uniqueness of the individual, identifying normative patterns of personal development and relationships, the reasons for deviant or abnormal behaviours and ways of 'reforming' the deviant (Woodroofe, 1962, Pearson, 1975). These issues are taken up in the following chapter. Both the method and the theories provided the opportunity of more systematic ways of continuing social work's concern with the 'character' of those in need of care and support and its claim to have a distinctive focus on the individual:

> Casework, then, is not merely a method or a means although, as has already been said, to the majority of social workers this is in truth all it implies. Were this so, there would be little to discuss. But it is because casework indicates definite and definable principles that the subject will remain of permanent importance, so long as human

beings remain as they are today; with sympathy and a desire to help individuals where luck seems out. And in mentioning individuals we begin to approach the root of the whole question: for casework is the outer sign of an inner faith — a faith which rests upon a belief in the individual and with the capacity of the individual to carve out his own life...

Casework then, becomes the antithesis of mass or socialistic measures, and the defender of casework finds that his plan will not rest merely on negating socialism but in proving that there is still much to be said for what can be described as individualism.

(Milnes, 1929, quoted in Walton, 1975, p. 150)

This sharp distinction between 'individualism' and 'socialism' had been a recurring theme in the development of social work as a way of identifying its special suitability as a form of social intervention and as a means of making clear how it was connected to the dominant ideologies of economic and political individualism. At the same time, the institutional basis of the various social works was changing, drawing workers into employment by the state, albeit still distributed across a wide range of different agencies and institutions. During the first half of the twentieth century, it was increasingly accepted that the institutional regimes of care and control (from asylum to the prison) needed workers who would try to manage the intersection between the internal life of the institution and life in the community. Thus medical almoners linked the patient in hospital with relatives and others outside, defining their role as working with people and their social networks rather than providing medical intervention. At the same time, there was a growing concern for workers who would select appropriate cases and work with them to keep them out of the institutions, whether the workhouse or the prison. In these contexts, casework functioned both as a method of assessment and intervention. It provided the basis for assessing the needs and character of the individual case and, through the agency and example of the case worker, was the means of helping and reforming the person in need.

In this growing intersection of social work and state institutions, it is possible to see two main tendencies which have continually characterized social work. On the one hand, the links to the institutions maintained the diversity of forms and sites of social work. On the other hand, the connections to the state established at least some of the conditions through which a tentative professional unity could be sought. As the welfare activities of both national and local government expanded during the inter-war years, so elements of social work were drawn into the operations of the state, albeit on a piecemeal basis. This unevenness should also alert us to the ways in which the different elements of social work were often allied to and dependent on other more highly professionalized practices. Thus, probation work was intimately bound up with the legal system and the other professions and occupations which operated within that system. Hospital almoners, by contrast, were operating on the margins of the medical and nursing professions, while mental health workers were in a field of practice dominated by the psychiatric profession. Each site, and each associated sphere of professional expertise thus gave a particular inflection to what social work meant in that context.

There were, however, attempts to create forms of professional unity above and beyond this diversity which highlighted similarities of method and knowledge that transcended the localized variations. The British Federation of Social Workers was formed in 1936 and struggled to create some sense of unity out of the diverse conditions of social work. The scale of the task may be measured from the constituent bodies who formed its original membership:

Association of Children's Care Committee Organizers

Association of Children's Moral Welfare Workers

Association of Family Caseworkers

Association of Occupational Therapists

Association of Psychiatric Social Workers

Royal College of Nursing (Public Health Section)

Association of Tuberculosis Care Committee Secretaries

Society of Women Housing Managers

Women Public Health Officers' Association

Association of Mental Health Workers

National Association of Probation Officers.
(Walton, 1975, pp. 154–5)

Most of these associations were themselves relatively newly created and the Federation had to confront tensions between the particular 'professionalizing' ambitions of each constituent body and the push towards a more generic professional unity for social work as a whole. This tension was to persist as a distinctive feature of social work through to the 1970s.

4   SOCIAL WORK AND THE STATE: THE FOUNDATION OF PROFESSIONAL BUREAUCRACIES

The growing involvement of the inter-war state in the institutional settings around which social work was practised and the tendency towards the paid employment of different groups of social workers established the conditions for the development of a particular type of professional. The dominant model of professions has always been that derived from the independent or 'collegial' professions of medicine and the law: self-regulating and claiming a distinctive knowledge and practice basis (Johnson, 1973). The growth of the state's social and welfare activities, however, provided the foundation for a different model of professionalism — based around the creation of a specific expertise and set of tasks based in a specific national or local government department. The leading example of this was the teaching profession but others were to follow as local government acquired an increasing range of welfare functions.

There were signs of these developments before 1945, particularly where some local authorities (subsequently labelled 'municipal labourist') began to develop more systematic programmes of welfare reform. The London County Council led by Herbert Morrison, which stressed increased house building and improved administration of health, education and the poor law, became one of the models developed further by the 1945–51 Labour government. Before 1945 the dominant understanding of the role of state employees had stressed the importance of effective administration. At a national level, the Civil Service embodied and expressed the assumption that competent generalist administrators were able to turn their hands to the supervision and administration of any particular activity with little difficulty. In local government, the key professions were those of law and accountancy, reflected in the dominant roles of town clerks and treasurers. Their principal tasks were to ensure that councils (or Boards of Guardians administering the Poor Law) did not exceed their legal powers or budgetary limits. Practical expertise in any of the welfare areas (health, education, housing, etc.) had none of the status of the established professions and offered little prospect of career development (Walton, 1975, Part II).

After 1945 there were efforts to make social and welfare provision by the state adopt a more systematic and organized form. This striving after consistency is apparent in all the reports and white papers of the period whether they cover social security, education or health. Alongside this is a view that the creation of such consistency in the provision of services requires the development of professions to sustain it. Such professionalism was seen to rest on the development of particular expertise, appropriate to the field of practice, rather than the 'generalist' approaches of the Civil Service. As the following extract on the development of a Ministry of Social Security in the 1940s makes clear, these new forms of 'trained expertise' are seen as essential to the remaking of welfare services:

> A Ministry of Social Security will have to maintain close contact with numerous individual citizens, each of whom will judge the Ministry chiefly by his reception at the local office. It is of paramount importance to the Ministry that he should be welcomed and treated with consideration and interest. The reputation of the Ministry will depend largely on its local staff. These will have to be selected and appointed carefully, and it is essential to consider at the outset what sort of people they must be...

These various functions need persons specially equipped for their performance — calculating widows' pensions rates, relating size of benefits to population groups, estimating the effect of industrial planning on the volume of claims national and local, talking with deserted wives or pushing the malingerer back to work — all these diverse jobs need special skills and special knowledge, and both at its Headquarters and in its local offices the Ministry must appoint appropriate persons to exercise appropriate sorts of skill.

This cuts right across existing Whitehall theories and procedures; there seems to be a Civil Service tradition that if you set up tidy governmental machinery and recruit a body of intelligent administrators of high integrity, you can run anything — shipping, Cairo, coal-mines, pensions. The needs of economic planning in a technical age may prove this thesis wrong. Already the majority of higher appointments outside the Civil Service call both for technical specialisation and for background knowledge of economic, sociological, psychological or scientific processes.

How are these sorts of experts to be got into the Ministry? In peacetime some of those who really understand the social services are congregated in the Universities; others are engaged on social surveys and research. Since the war many of them are temporary civil servants; they have been called in not only because administration has increased in scope, but because the urgency of war-time planning calls for the right people in the right places. If later we are to plan for national well-being the same criterion must carry over. We must have first-class persons where their skills are needed. We must be prepared to take economists, sociologists, psychologists and statisticians into the Ministry of Social Security at the higher salary ranges as temporary staff. We must be prepared to use suitable experts wherever they are to be found in the community...

Recognition of the need for social science experts must be established straight away so that they may be incorporated into the new Ministry as soon as it is formed. 'Good administrators' brought in from the higher ranks of other Ministries to start the new one will not suffice. It is essential that at least some of those who administer at the highest levels should understand the nature and the purpose of the social services.

(Clarke, 1943, pp. 373–5, 376–7)

These arguments highlight the importance of developing trained experts as the basis for state welfare and were widely echoed in discussions about the recruitment and training of social workers in the post-war period (The Younghusband Report, 1959; Rodgers and Dixon, 1960). Such developments emphasized the necessity of creating recognizable clusters of professionalized 'expertise' for welfare services, especially given the relative lack of relevant training and qualifications. Equally, the expansion and creation of nationally organized frameworks for service delivery created the conditions for further professional development. It has been argued by some authors that the very structures of the welfare state were shaped by the demands of embryonic professional or occupational groups to provide themselves with relatively privileged positions within the post-war labour market (e.g., Reade, 1987, Chapter 2). Whether one views the state or the occupational groups as the driving force, it is clear that the intersection of these processes created the conditions for a distinctive new type of professionalism — 'bureaucratic professionalism' — in which professional expertise is practised within the complex administrative structure and within the statutory frameworks of a department of central or local government (Mintzberg, 1983; see also Johnson, 1973, who uses the term 'mediating professions'). In the post-war context, the state needed the development of such 'bureaucratic professions' to staff the expansion of welfare departments while the would-be professions benefited from the occupational and organizational base provided by the state:

> The new bureaucratic professions...do not resist the extension of state power...for they have no choice but to be public employees. On the contrary, they generally welcome the extension of state power, for it is the only source of such power as they themselves possess; indeed, these occupational groups owe their very existence to the power of the state.
>
> (Reade, 1987, p. 126)

Social work in the two decades after the Second World War made steady advances in these conditions — with growing numbers being employed in welfare work and with some expansion of professional training. Nonetheless, such progress was overshadowed by the fragmented character of social work — still split into diverse forms, practised in different institutions, based in different departments and for which different types of training were being provided. In the interwar years, the sectors associated with established professions (medicine and law) had taken leading roles in trying to shape the creation of a professionalized social work. Hospital almoners, mental health workers, psychiatric social workers and the Probation Service had all tried to develop quasi-professional associations and argued for the need for training and qualifications. In the 1950s, however, the balance of occupational power began to shift after the creation of local authority Children's Departments by the 1948 Children Act which followed on Reports from the Clyde Committee (Scotland) and the Curtis Committee (England and Wales) in 1946. Children's Departments increasingly became the focal point for the arguments about how to unify social work which culminated in the 'generic' reorganizations of the 1970s (discussed further in Chapter 3).

We need to note one further feature of the 'professionalizing' trend within social work during the 1950s and 1960s. Up to this point, social work in all its forms had been a predominantly female occupation — both in its voluntary and paid employment varieties. One of the arguments which supported 'professionalism', and especially the creation of departments which required qualified workers with proper career structures, was the importance of opening the field of social work to men who, it was felt, were dissuaded by the poor conditions and prospects of welfare work. As the scale of the different departments employing welfare workers expanded, and in the process senior and managerial positions were created, such senior positions became disproportionately filled by men with the exception of the new Children's Departments (Walton, 1975, Chapter 15).

5   SOCIAL WORK AND SOCIAL ORDER

This brief consideration of social work's development from the 1860s to the 1960s has highlighted a number of themes which are central to the more recent fortunes of social work and which are explored more extensively in the following chapters. At this point, though, it is worth extracting these themes from their historical setting and considering their implications in more general terms.

The first of these themes concerns social work's propensity to view social problems in an individualized way: to give priority to both explanations and remedies at the level of the individual. Perhaps more accurately, this should be termed the level of the individual/family complex, given that the family has been a central focus of social work intervention. To some extent, this individual/familial focus reflects the importance of psychological theories and approaches in the development of social work, and this is explored further in Chapter 2. But this dominant focus in social work preceded the systematic elaboration of psychology as an academic discipline. Both social work's social origins and its place within wider patterns of social organization have played a part in shaping this individual/familial concentration. The mid-nineteenth century stress on personal contact across the classes in charitable work produced an emphasis on the importance of one individual relating to and assisting another. This approach laid great emphasis on understanding the unique circumstances and character of the person to be assisted. Such scrutiny of the individual was also seen as essential for the evaluation of the person to be helped. This detailed attention provided the means by which those genuinely in need and deserving help could be distinguished from the undeserving. The development of these concerns into 'systematic casework' placed a stress on the uniqueness of the individual at the heart of social work practice. Both evaluation and assistance were framed in individualized terms.

In this way, proponents of social work were able to distinguish their approach from social reform or socialism (as in the quotation from Milnes earlier in this chapter). At best, social rather than individual reform represented a different approach to social problems, concerned with the 'mass' rather than the individual. More frequently, the early proponents of social work viewed social reform as a political danger which could undermine social order. As more collective welfare measures gained political legitimacy in the early twentieth century, this stark distinction between 'individualistic' and 'socialistic' approaches diminished in intensity. Instead social work was defended and promoted as possessing a distinctive concern with and sensitivity to the individual which other welfare measures lacked.

In practice, the distinction proved still harder to maintain. The daily encounter with poverty and need which characterized the working life of social workers led at least some of them to question the individual/familial focus and look to more structural remedies for social problems. Despite this tension within social work, the predominant focus of theory and practice has remained that of the individual/familial complex. Nevertheless, as subsequent chapters show, the individual-social tension has persisted as one thread within social work's more recent development.

The second theme which needs to be drawn out is the relationship between social work and power. Social work's origins lie in specific patterns of class power, in particular the unequal distribution of social and economic resources. Charity involved a cautious and conditional act of redistribution towards those in need. The conditions of redistribution were intended to ensure that only certain categories of people benefited and that those who benefited would learn the appropriate social lessons from the encounter.

In such contexts, the specific power associated with social work came to be that of 'gatekeepers' controlling access to resources. Casework, as we have seen, developed as a way of evaluating those in need and deciding who should be allowed resources and under what conditions. These patterns of power applied not only to the obvious material resources of money and goods, but to more intangible resources as well. For example, the forerunners of the Probation Service, in collaboration with the courts, exercised influence over the form and nature of punishments, particularly over whether imprisonment or supervision in the community would be the outcome.

These powers of resource control were supplemented by other forms of power during the development of social work. One of these was the result of social workers' attachment to other institutions (prisons, courts, hospitals, etc.). In these settings, the social workers' role as supports or adjuncts to other professions (the law, medicine and psychiatry) gave social workers a derived or secondary authority. Alongside this, efforts to professionalize social work tried to stress its own unique and distinctive approach to theory and practice. Laying claim to a distinctive expertise involved a bid for social and professional power in a context where the post-war expansion of the welfare state placed a premium on the role of professionalized expertise.

The central focus of these forms of power was located in the relationships between social workers and the people who formed their cases. Such relationships were structurally unequal in three respects. The first was the position of social workers as gatekeepers to resources which were valued or needed by the 'clients' (to adopt the term of professionalism).

The second occurred in those contexts where clients were required by law to have a social worker and the relationship provided social workers with statutory powers over their 'clients'. Third, the claim to 'expertise' involved a different sort of power: the claim that experts must necessarily know better than those who are not experts and thus that their judgements should be trusted and followed. Again, subsequent chapters will explore the significance of power in the later development of social work.

The third, and final, theme concerns the relationship between social work and patterns of social inequality. Social work came to occupy an ambiguous relationship to social inequalities. Emerging as it did as a form of intervention directed at the poorest and neediest in society, the issues of social inequality could hardly be avoided. Its origins remind us that it was never intended to be a practice which would remedy or reform structural inequality. On the contrary, it was directed at alleviating individual misery or misfortune, or at least to helping the unfortunate to help themselves. As we saw earlier, the individualism of social work was championed as an explicit alternative to 'socialist' measures directed at more structural reform.

In that sense, social work was dominated by an impetus to help individuals adjust to wider social arrangements: to learn to lead 'good and useful lives' according to the prevailing social norms. In the process, of course, social workers had to address the problem that the mass of misery and misfortune which they encountered in their case loads amounted to more than could be explained by individual circumstances. As a result, there were intermittent attempts to change the relationship between social work and inequality: to link social work and social reform, to 'take the side' of the poor or oppressed or to demand more structural changes. Such efforts, however, took place at the edges rather than at the centre of social work. In general terms, we might say that social work has tended to reproduce rather than redress social inequality.

This is not to question the compassion, care and concern of individual social workers, or to suggest that individuals have not been helped by the interventions of social workers. But it is important to recognize that the position and role of social work as a social intervention was dominated by pressures to separate the alleviation of individual misery from concerns with structural inequality. This structuring of social work established constraints and limitations on the forms of help and intervention that were available to social workers. This was true not just in relation to the most obvious patterns of material inequality, but in relation to other forms of social division, too. Conventional social norms about work, the family, the care of children, ethnicity and sexuality were replicated within the theories and orientations of social work. The result was that social work interventions were profoundly shaped by these assumptions and tried to reproduce them in practice. These issues about the place of social work in reproducing social divisions will be taken up in later chapters. At this point, it is important to register just how deeply this tendency towards the reproduction of social divisions and forms of inequality was locked into the 'mission' of social work. This mission centred on helping individuals to function more effectively in their social environment. The logic was to reform the individual (by overcoming what was preventing them behaving like 'normal' individuals) rather than to reform the social environment.

6   CAUGHT IN THE MIDDLE?

One conclusion to draw from this chapter is that social work is a peculiar and ambiguous practice: born out of concern with human suffering but with its face firmly set against changing social patterns which might be the cause of suffering. Such ambiguities or tensions were present at the moment of social work's birth and have continued to exercise a considerable influence over its subsequent development.

It is worth reflecting briefly on some of these ambiguities and the conflicting pressures which created them. We might begin with the complex motivations behind nineteenth century charity: the mixture of compassion and fear discussed earlier. Compassion drove the efforts to provide help and assistance to the 'unfortunate'. Fear prescribed the limits and conditions to such assistance. Unconditional charity was seen as a recipe for social chaos so it was necessary to evaluate the 'cases' and select only the deserving. It was also necessary to monitor and supervise their progress and assess their degree of conformity to social expectations.

From the outset, then, casework was intrusive. For systematic intervention, the life, manners and habits of the 'case' had to be investigated so that their character could be evaluated. Alongside this went the commitment to the value of a *personalized* relationship between the worker and the case: the undertaking to 'advise, assist and befriend' that defined the responsibilities of probation workers in the 1907 Probation of Offenders Act. This tangled complex of compassion and fear is more often addressed as the interlinking of 'care and control' in social work: the provision of a personalized assistance uneasily combined with powers to evaluate, direct and make decisions affecting the client's life.

This complex motivation and the complicated casework relationship to which it gave rise is intimately linked to another area of social work's ambiguity. Social workers have always been expected to balance the claims of the client's needs with the needs of society. To some extent, this balance has been resolved by assuming that the client's needs and society's needs are not in tension: restoring the client to 'normal functioning' satisfies everyone's interests. At other times, social workers have been less willing to accept this assumption of harmonious interests and have tried to redefine their role as the champion or advocate of the client. In other circumstances, social workers have insisted that, although clients may think they know what their needs are, social workers as society's expert representatives know better. Perhaps more importantly, they have the power to make their definition of the client's needs stick.

There is a connection here with a further area of ambiguity concerning social work's individual forms. From its origins, social work has been championed as having a distinctive concern with individuals and their unique circumstances and characters. At the same time, the varieties of social work have been trying to evaluate those individuals to see where they fit into a limited range of categories. Originally, this related to simple categories of 'deserving' or 'undeserving' (whether for charitable assistance or being released on probation). The greater involvement of social work with state welfare may have made the categories more complicated, but social workers still had to confront the task of assessing whether the client met the necessary professional or legislative definition of 'need'. These evaluative tasks made social work both highly personalized and highly impersonal. The social worker negotiated this ambiguity, linking the 'unique' individual to the categorizations of need and assistance.

These are ambiguities within social work: tensions which have made the practice of social work fraught with potential difficulties for social workers. But social work is ambiguous in a further sense. This ambiguity is reflected in the difficulty of defining what social work *is*, as opposed to enumerating a list of things that social workers *do*. The brief history presented in this chapter suggests some reasons for this ambiguity. The origins of what we now call social work are to be found in the activities of different groups and agencies working in a variety of different settings. They had two things in common: their development on the margins of other social institutions and their emphasis on a personalized relationship of care and control (the casework method). The development of social work was marked by this tension between difference (different institutions, different 'client groups', different 'problems' and relationships with different professions) on the one hand and the common method on the other. The casework method and all that it implies became the 'common core' around which attempts to create a unified social work profession took shape. The commitment to casework was seen as summarizing a number of different elements: the focus on the individual/family complex; the salience of psychological approaches as a professional knowledge-base; and the combination of evaluation and assistance in a personalized relationship. Attempts to build a professional unity around this common commitment to casework were recurrently confronted by the pressures of 'difference'. This tension between difference and unity was not resolved until the late 1960s, and is discussed further in Chapter 3. Both social work and the experience of those practising it may be described as being 'caught in the middle' of conflicting pressures and demands. This chapter has concentrated on how such pressures were established in the early development of social work. Later chapters explore how the pressures and demands to which social work is subject have changed.

REFERENCES

Bochel, D. (1976) *Probation and After-Care: Its Development in England and Wales*, Edinburgh, Scottish Academic Press.

Clarke, J.S. (1943) 'The staff problem' in W.A. Robson (ed.) *Social Security*, London, Allen and Unwin.

Clyde Committee (1946) *The Report of the Committee on Homeless Children*, CM 6911, London, HMSO.

Curtis Committee (1946) *The Report of the Committee on the Care of Children*, CM 6922, London, HMSO.

Henriques, U. (1979) *Before the Welfare State*, London, Longman.

Johnson, T. (1973) *Professions and Power*, London, Macmillan.

Melossi, D. and Pavarini, M. (1981) *The Prison and the Factory*, Basingstoke, Macmillan.

Milnes, S. (1929) 'The difficulties encountered in recruiting and training voluntary and professional workers in a social case agency', *COS Quarterly*, January.

Mintzberg, H. (1983) *Structure in Fives: Designing Effective Organizations*, Englewood Cliffs, N.J., Prentice Hall.

Mort, F. (1987) *Dangerous Sexualities: Medico-Moral Politics in England since 1830*, London, Routledge and Kegan Paul.

Murphy, J. (1992) *Origins of Social Work Services — Scottish Dimensions*, Edinburgh, Scottish Academic Press.

Pearson, G. (1975) *The Deviant Imagination*, London, Macmillan.

Reade, E. (1987) *British Town and Country Planning*, Buckingham, Open University Press.

Rodgers, B.N. and Dixon, J. (1960) *A Portrait of Social Work*, Oxford, Oxford University Press.

Steadman-Jones, G. (1971) *Outcast London*, Oxford, Oxford University Press.

Walton, R. (1975) *Women in Social Work*, London, Routledge and Kegan Paul.

Woodroofe, K. (1962) *From Charity to Social Work*, London, Routledge and Kegan Paul.

Young, A.F. and Ashton, E.T. (1956) *British Social Work in the Nineteenth Century*, London, Routledge and Kegan Paul.

Younghusband, E. (1951) *Social Work in Britain*, London, Constable.

Younghusband Report, The (1959) *Report of the Working Party on Social Workers in the Local Authority Health and Welfare Services*, London, HMSO.

STUDY QUESTIONS

1 Why did social work develop around concerns for both care and control?

2 What was distinctive about social work as a form of social intervention?

3 What are the implications of social work's focus on individuals?

4 What problems were associated with attempts to unify social work?

5 How would you characterize social work's relationship with patterns of social inequality?

CHAPTER 2
UNDERSTANDING PEOPLE: THE GROWTH OF AN EXPERTISE

ROGER SAPSFORD

> Psychology, like all the other sciences, has as its main aim the
> prediction of future behaviour in the system observed. That it can
> never predict in detail is irrelevant, since it is sufficient that we can
> predict probable trends...The psychologist...aims to investigate
> human behaviour with a view to discovering its underlying causes;
> for it is only be dealing with causes that we can hope to influence
> future behaviour if and when this becomes necessary.
>
> (Brown, 1954, pp. 287–8)

This chapter begins our discussion of professional practice and professional power by looking at a 'knowledge-base' which has united different varieties of professionals who have responsibility for people. It is
much influenced by the ideas of Foucault and the work of Nikolas Rose
(1985, 1989) and Wendy Hollway (1991). In it I shall survey the growth
and implications of what Rose has called 'The Psychology Complex', the
network of ideas about the nature of human beings, their perfectibility or
corrigibility, the reasons for their behaviour and the ways in which they
may be classified, selected and/or controlled. What I am trying to unpick
is the complex layers of meaning within which the modern social worker,
health visitor, therapist, psychologist or school teacher works. There is no
intention to write a 'history of ideas'; our concern will be more with the
practices and institutions which give substance to the ideas while being
moulded by them.

At the core of this 'Psychology Complex' is a picture of the human and
social being as intrinsically individual — to be understood as a locus
which receives experience and emits behaviour. This is not, of course, an
invention of psychology, but rather a precondition allowing certain kinds
of psychology to flourish; it is a 'model of the person' characteristic of
capitalist socio-economic organization. (Psychology has reinforced it and
legitimated it, however.) We tend to take the extreme individualism of our
society for granted, as an uncontroversial representation of reality, but it
is by no means the only way of modelling the social world. Cross-cultural-
ly, it can be shown that alternative ways of viewing the person are possible which put less stress on individuality. Historically even within our
own culture it has seemed as plausible to describe the human species as
essentially and instinctively social as to characterize it as made up of
individuals in competition.

The second core feature of the discourse is that it 'sees' the individual in
turn as made up of — 'possessing' — qualities which are measurable and
which enable us to compare one individual with another. In the early

forms the discourse is concerned with physical and to a lesser extent moral qualities; in later and more developed forms it centres on psychological qualities — mental abilities, emotional tendencies, degrees and kinds of motivation, the extent of types of learning, and so on. During the period of industrialization a new knowledge-base grew up around this increasingly dominant view of human nature — what eventually became the disciplines of 'individual' and 'social' psychology. Terms were developed in which to describe the human subject, and concepts developed in these terms, which allowed the measurement of the subject's 'interior state'. This leads us to the third core feature, that the discourse is mostly aimed at the *management* of the individual. Mostly it posits human beings who are perfectible or changeable or curable, by manipulation of their qualities or attributes.

Beyond these core features, considerable diversity is to be found. In all the variants, however, the discourse defines individuals rather than social units as the appropriate object of study, and in almost all the variants the purpose of study is explicitly or implicitly to modify these individuals in the interests of social order and/or industrial production. Within the broad range of approaches there is room for a wide variety of particular 'schools'; several different and apparently opposed psychological theories may be seen as expressing the same discourse. The discourse does not determine which school of psychology shall win any given debate. What it does determine is the terms in which the debate shall be conducted: the social world shall be characterized in terms of individuals and their interactions, the individuals shall be amenable to further simplification into underlying qualities or tendencies of a more general nature (the particular individual being seen as embodying a particular combination of these qualities or tendencies), and the underlying purpose of analysis shall be the prediction and/or manipulation of the individual's behaviour.

I shall not concern myself here with the truth or falsity of the psychological knowledge-base which is under discussion; it is not the purpose of this chapter to express approval or disapproval of any part of it. Psychology is as it is, and if it were not, then some other body of knowledge would undoubtedly fulfil a similar function — perhaps less effectively and with less benefit to the individuals to whom it is applied. Nor am I concerned, for the most part, with the motives or probity of practitioners. There can be little doubt that most practitioners subscribe to a purpose of which we would approve — to help people to improve themselves, or to fit them to live in the social world without undue misery, or to prevent them from destroying a social order which benefits the majority of us in some sense. Psychology and the allied disciplines influenced by it are thus much concerned with the management of people, but it should not be supposed that the motivation of the practitioners is Machiavellian — totally at the service of management and government. Psychology's much wider aim is to serve *all* its clients by enabling them to achieve the happiness/contentment/fulfilment which is reached when we perform to the best of our capabilities. It can, in principle, be used just as readily to empower individuals as to control them — *provided* that they are content with the way in which it defines them and their powers and wants.

It also needs to be pointed out, perhaps, that it is not an attack on a particular discourse, nor is it an attack on those whose professional position is underpinned by that discourse, to show that it embodies and is used to further a form of social control. *All* social relations embody social controls; the question is not *whether* social control is an element, but *what* social control. What is under discussion here is the way of looking at people and their relationships, and at the social structures/processes which they embody and by which they are constrained. The aim of this chapter is not to criticize, but to 'make strange' some of what we take for granted about people and to try to understand it better by looking at its origins, development and functions and the ways in which it leads 'naturally' to particular ways of maintaining social order.

I   THE NATION'S CHILDREN

It was during the Victorian era in Britain that middle-class people in both national government and local government began to conceive of 'the populace' (working-class people) not just as a rabble or a source of labour but as a national resource. Various fears — about the fitness of working-class youths for army recruitment, the size and efficiency of the army (in the aftermath of unexpected defeats in for example the Sudan), the efficiency of British factories and shipyards in the face of competition from Germany and the United States — began to focus attention on children as the next generation of workers and soldiers and in a literal sense the future of the Empire. Empire and 'race' were confounded in Victorian rhetoric, and social theories modelled on the biological theories of Darwin saw 'races' as in social competition to survive and expand. There was also substantial concern over the differential breeding rate by class, with middle-class families at the turn of the century having fewer children than working-class ones. The scientists of the time took this as indicating the potential for degeneration in the 'national breeding stock', and the unfitness of so many for military service at the time of the Boer War was taken as evidence that such degeneration was indeed taking place.

The practical action that was taken was to target mothers — specifically, working-class mothers — and through them to try to improve the health of children. Medical men exhorted, and a cadre of voluntary visiting ladies travelled the working-class areas preaching hygiene and good household management. These 'sanitary missionaries' — at first recruited from the same ranks as the lady missionaries who took biblical tracts round to working-class homes — came to be employed and paid as family visitors or health visitors, and gradually the state took over responsibility for their employment and training. At the turn of the century, it was mainly working-class mothers who came to their attention, and among them mainly women who had paid employment outside the home and could thus be seen as neglecting what the middle classes had come to see as 'the duties of motherhood'. Gradually, under state control, they became responsible for the surveillance of the health of all young children and the competence of all mothers.

The fear of riot and degeneration in the populace was very real in the nineteenth century, with the example of the French Revolution not far in the past. Although by the end of the century the fear of mob riot had declined, it came to be replaced by a fear of national degeneration. When the scientists and politicians of the time saw the labouring classes, the criminals, the prostitutes, the physically disabled and the mentally deficient breeding at a faster rate than the productive and responsible classes, they could not but fear for the future of the nation. Such fears were fuelled by a science that had discovered the principles of inheritance and believed in the possibility of a literal degeneration of bloodlines — that the children of criminals or paupers could well be mentally defective, so that a 'taint' could be passed on into the national stock by their breeding. People of mild mental disability were particularly feared, because they were relatively invisible — they did not stand out as adults. (The introduction of universal schooling just before the turn of the century demonstrated just how many children there were who appeared not to be able to cope with it, and the numbers were a great cause for concern.) In 1883 the noted psychologist Francis Galton was preaching the control of breeding without attracting much attention, but by 1904 Karl Pearson, one of the fathers of intelligence testing, was arguing a similar case to much more receptive audiences. An early draft of the 1913 Mental Health Act contained a clause forbidding the marriage of the feeble-minded and permitting compulsory sterilization. This was not, in the end, passed into law, but it came very close to it; the notion that people with learning difficulties should be sterilized has recurred from time to time during the century (see for example Board of Control, 1934).

The work of psychologists in the early years of the century came as a partial answer to some of these fears. The first workable scale of general intelligence — a test purporting to discriminate badly schooled children from the unschoolable — was developed by Binet and Simon in France in the early years of the century. This, developed further by other psychologists in England and the United States, provided an instrument which could be used to distinguish those with learning difficulties from the 'normal' child, and a way of establishing what was to count as normal or abnormal in the matter of mental ability. It also had the effect, as its use became popular, of taking some of the control of children and childhood out of the hands of medical doctors and presenting it to a newly formed professional class of psychologists. The monitoring of young babies for signs of handicap made it necessary for health visitors (and doctors) to include some elements of psychology in their training and adopt it as part of their professional expertise.

The family discourse of 'a mother and her children' determined that it was mothers who were responsible to the nation for the physical and moral health of their children, and the health visiting service grew up at least in part to oversee their responsibility for the former. In the years up to the First World War, those who advised and monitored mothers on the well-being of their children were predominantly medical men, or medically trained and/or supervised, and the information which was expressed related predominantly to physical medicine and physical hygiene. Mothers were conceptualized to an extent as agents of the state, responsible for the well-being of the state's children, and their capacity to carry out this task was monitored and reinforced by doctors, health visitors and state and voluntary agencies within the medical fold. Society required the labour of mothers, but mothers also stood to gain from their relationship with the outreaching arms of medicine. It was during this period that mothers came to be seen as the experts on children — with medical advice when needed — and their position within the structure of the family benefited from this enhancement of their status.

From that time on into the 1960s, however, a different kind of 'medicine' evolved around a different view of how the child developed into a person. The 'individual' psychology of mental traits and psychometric measurement, coupled with Freudian and other 'psychiatric' ideas about the formative role of a child's early years, gave us a new view of humankind, and also a new kind of expert. In this picture of development the passage from child to healthy adult was more precarious than had previously been argued, and the child was much more vulnerable in the early years than had previously been supposed. This development of discourse brought about a fundamental change in the implicit contract between the state and mothers, because the task which they were now set became, even in principle, impossible to fulfil completely. Child rearing became a difficult and problematic full-time job, involving day-to-day responsibility for the child's thoughts and feelings as well as for his or her physical health.

In the 1920s and 1930s the concern with the fitness of children began to widen, from physical, intellectual and moral fitness to mental fitness, based on psychological theories of how adult mental disturbance is the result of deviant or inadequate family care in childhood. Between the two 'great wars' a psychology developed which considered ways in which the mother's aberrant views and attitudes were conveyed to the child and the parents' disharmonies provided an unsettling and unsound 'symbolic environment'. After the Second World War this was reworked and retheorized by cross-fertilization with the tradition of psychoanalysis which had by then been active in England for some thirty years, to put greater emphasis on the emotional and relational environment (as something through and against which the child had to mature in psychic terms). This meant greater emphasis being placed on the vital importance of the mother and her love for the child. Influential writers and popularizers such as Bowlby and Winnicott managed to convince a generation of mothers that their first duty was to the child. They also convinced a generation of experts.

The mother's duty, then, became to take responsibility for every aspect of the child. Sexuality, sanity, social competence, achievement and capability: these are all the mother's responsibility to establish and monitor in the child, in the sense that it is the mother who will most likely be blamed if anything goes wrong. In turn the need for expert guidance became even clearer, as each new development of 'mother/child science' was taken up by the experts — by doctors and thence by health visitors, and by social workers via child psychologists and their courses of training. The new knowledge was complex and far ranging, and the new task was effectively so all-encompassing as to be beyond the scope of any one person. The task of overseeing child development reaches into every aspect of life, and every unconsidered action or inaction may later be identified as a cause of later inadequacies.

Because *everyone* can in some sense be described as inadequate, there can never be evidence that parents have unequivocally succeeded in their child-rearing task. (The characteristic stance of mothers in this half of the century, therefore, has probably been one of guilt.) Mothers have become responsible for their children's health, their sanity, their happiness, their behaviour as children and their future adequacy as adults. Everything their children do or experience comes to be seen as shaping emotions and/ or mentality, and so everything the children do or experience becomes something for which the mother may later be blamed. The mother calls on outside experts and agencies for help and advice, and comes to be subordinate to them as the task which she is called on to carry out becomes one of ever increasing and bewildering complexity. It is she who is the target of agencies which were set up to monitor the behaviour of working-class women and came eventually to monitor the behaviour of all. It is she who is the intermediary between the child, the school and other state agencies — the contact point, the conduit and, if need be, the scapegoat, controlled in this role as much by her own feelings of guilt and inadequacy as by any external blame.

Outside the family, as Britain became increasingly a disciplined industrial society, schooling became an increasingly important part of the state/ societal mechanism for controlling children and preparing them as future workers and managers. School was seen as establishing 'habits of industry' in children, accustoming them to systematic routine and making them come to regard it as a normal way of life, along with obedience to appointed authority. A further benefit of schooling was that its apparent openness concealed the mechanisms of stratification. Working-class children tended on the whole to receive a very different schooling from middle-class ones, but nonetheless their success or failure in the educational system (which acted and still acts as a passport to types of employment) could be seen as due to their efforts and abilities or lack of effort and ability, even by the children themselves.

In all this, achievement and intelligence testing acted as an important 'objective' measure and justification for the child's destination in life. By about 1925 the stratification of schools into 'academic' and 'vocational' was well advanced, with intelligence tests coming into prominence as one way of determining which track should be followed. With the 1944 Education Act a tripartite system of grammar, technical and secondary modern schooling was set up in many areas, and intelligence tests were a major part of the selection mechanism. In Scotland, the 1945 Education Act established a bipartite division, at age 11, between Senior and Junior Secondary Schools. Within each track achievement testing acted in the same way — to differentiate, classify and assign pupils, and to justify their assignment in their own eyes. With the proliferation of 'comprehensive' schooling in the last two decades we appear superficially to have retreated from the clear differentiation of pupils by educational level which was practised in the 1950s and 1960s, but vocational tracking still occurs within these schools and children are still judged and assigned on the basis of intelligence and achievement. The political rhetoric on education which is current at the time of writing appears, if anything, to reinforce the old values. 'Equality of opportunity' is used in justification of uniform national curricula and the close monitoring of teacher performance. The structural changes to the education system, however, in terms of allowing individual schools more control over the selection of pupils and more opportunity to specialize in what they offer, would appear to foreshadow the reintroduction of a stratified schooling system and is justified at least in part as an efficient way of maximizing the future performance of the nation's children as workers.

Thus within the schooling system we can see what we might call a 'double psychologization' at work. Psychological concepts are called into play to categorize deviant children — children with 'learning difficulties' and children with 'behavioural problems' — and to suggest ways of treating or managing them. More widely, however, the whole population of children comes to be 'subjects of psychology', to be categorized, and managed according to their category. Even when intelligence tests are not employed, the concept of children as more or less intellectually able, and of intellectual ability as something to be fostered in them, has come to dominate the way in which we think of schooling and the ways in which we organize it.

Psychological and psychiatric ways of understanding the 'disturbed' child penetrate two major institutions — the schools and the courts — in a slightly different way but within the same overall conceptual framework. 'The maladjusted child' (or similar formulations) began to appear as a label within the school system from about the end of the First World War. Child Guidance Clinics grew up during the 1920s and 1930s to deal with behavioural problems identified at school, in the same way that the School Medical Service dealt with physical problems. In practice this gave a way of redefining the difficult child as in need of professional control, and psychology and psychiatry provided the knowledge-base which legitimated that definition. A second point of application was to juvenile delinquents themselves.

In the second half of the nineteenth century separate provision from what was used for adults was made for two important classes of children: children who had committed criminal offences and could be expected to continue doing so if left to themselves, and children seen as 'in danger' (the homeless, those neglected or brutalized by their parents, and those lacking discipline in the home). A series of Acts of Parliament established where such children could be 're-socialized' in a substitute family and taught 'habits of industry'. The Children's Act of 1908 extended the provision into the community, allowing those who might have been sent away to be released on their own promise of good behaviour and subject to a period of supervision by a probation officer. The Act also set up juvenile courts to further separate children from adult offenders, a principle subsequently adopted in Scotland following the 1932 Children and Young Persons Act. The juvenile courts brought within the ambit and powers of the criminal law the supervision of families with adolescent children, which health visitors carried out, with fewer powers on families with young children; being 'in need of care and control' brought a child within the powers of the courts just as surely as a criminal offence.

The burgeoning field of forensic examination and treatment was firmly claimed by the discipline of 'individual' psychology — foremost among whose exponents at the time was Cyril Burt. In his book *The Young Delinquent*, first published in 1925 but accepted as an authoritative source for twenty years thereafter, Burt looked to explain the varieties of delinquency and to suggest ways of treating them. He allowed that some children might be 'emotionally defective', but for the majority he posited causal events in their early lives and saw part of psychology's task as elucidating these events — for the offender as well as for the psychologist — and helping to set up new patterns of life. Though this approach to crime — seeing it as a property of individuals and due to faulty socialization — is currently out of favour in academic criminology, to this day it retains its hold on those who are caring for young people or training to do so. In a popular textbook for care assistants and residential social workers, for example, we find it asserted:

> A child may well lack the material things of life and have some degree of social disadvantage, but she may be well loved and cared for... But what of the child without that loving care, the child who suffers emotional disadvantages and deprivations? ...If we look at children who get themselves into trouble...we find that the greatest number do come from backgrounds that are both emotionally and socially disadvantaged.
>
> (Summer, 1981, pp. 42–3).

Thus in this section we have traced the development of a view of the child as a vital resource to be conserved and a fragile developing creature to be steered and managed — and, if need be, salvaged and reconstituted — towards competent adult function in an industrialized and class-divided world. We have seen that the responsibility for most of the child's constitution is placed firmly within the family and specifically in the hands of the mother. It is this responsibility which helps to constitute modern motherhood as what it is — a potentially infinite task and source of deep feelings of guilt and inadequacy, as well as a set of social expectations. The responsibility is carried out under regular surveillance by health visitors, doctors and teachers, and according to the precepts of a range of experts, among whom psychologists predominate. The development of applied psychology and its tendency to locate social problems as 'properties' of individuals, caused by faulty training (or sometimes biological inadequacy), have been illustrated, as has the tendency to locate problem individuals *as* problems precisely because they diverge from a norm. It remains, in the rest of the chapter, to extend our glance to look at psychology's impact on aspects of adult life.

2   RECLAIMING THE DERELICT

> Social work theory...should serve the following functions: it should provide some explanation for the complexities we observe in our practice so that out of apparent chaos we might expose patterns and regularities in behaviour and situations: it should therefore help us to predict future behaviour, and how the problem or condition could develop and what might be the effect of planned change.
>
> (Coulshead, 1991, p. 8)

In this section the 'subjects' are individuals characterized by the social system as deviants — the poor, the unemployed and, as a more extreme deviation, people in prison. The process which is examined is one of reclaiming them for the norm of respectable employed life. Attitudes to the punishment of serious crime show very clearly how subjects become 'psychologized'. Over a comparatively short period, penal practice changed from violent exemplary punishment to deter other potential offenders to the creation of 'reformatories' for rehabilitating offenders and re-fitting them for 'normal life'. In the world outside the prison the changes are not as sudden or noticeable, but a trend may be traced from a view of the socially inadequate as responsible for his or her own condition and capable, with supervision, of changing it, to a characterization of him or her as in some way 'damaged' and in need of 'repair'. In other words, we can detect the psychologization of the subject, in the limited sense in which the term has been used in this chapter — the maintenance of individual responsibility, but a view of social inadequacy as a condition caused by a potentially curable imbalance of internal states which can be remedied or controlled by professional intervention. This section traces these changes and the correlated growth and consolidation of the social work profession as agents of change, and also the way that this profession validates and is validated by psychological 'knowledge'.

Paupers were regulated in the early years of the eighteenth century by Poor Laws which dated from 1597 in Scotland and 1601 in England. The English Act restricted the movement of the indigent but provided allowances based on the cost of food and the size of the family which was to be fed. Both these principles were attacked in the nineteenth century — the former as restricting the mobility of labour and therefore artificially constricting the market, and the latter as putting a premium on family size and encouraging the lowest strata to breed. The new Poor Laws which followed on the Chadwick Report in 1834 (see Poor Law Commission, 1834) had as their central tenet the principle of 'less eligibility' — that relief for the poor should be so planned that those in the worst paid jobs were still better off than those on relief. Indeed, a punitive element was implicit in the legislation; there was an intention that paupers should suffer for their condition. Two kinds of relief were offered — 'indoor' and 'outdoor'. 'Indoor relief' meant committal to the workhouse, to be fed and boarded in return for productive labour — designed as a test of the reality of need, for conditions were unpleasant enough that no-one who had an alternative would choose this one. 'Outdoor relief' was paid to recipients who continued to live in their own homes. A rigid distinction was made between those in genuine need and those who were seen as using the system in some way to avoid work. In between came those who — from choice or from necessity — had no regular employment but subsisted on casual labour. The able-bodied unemployed tended to be seen as rogues in need of discipline, and the totally unemployable as degenerates to be separated from the rest of the population before they contaminated it. The presumption was guilt until innocence was proved: it was assumed that pauperism was the result of improvidence or unwillingness to work, unless the contrary could be demonstrated. Age or mental condition was no excuse. The workhouses were not just or even mainly forced labour camps for the able-bodied. They quickly filled up with orphans, the elderly, the sick and disabled, the mentally ill and those who would now be described as having 'learning difficulties'.

The urban pauper and vagrant was of even greater concern to the Victorians than his or her rural counterpart. People without jobs were attracted into the cities in the hope of easy money, or travelled there in the vain hope of finding work, and large 'rookeries' developed in which the very poor lived in total squalor alongside criminals and prostitutes — to the extent that these three groups were not all represented in the same people. It was the fear of the urban pauper as much as anything that led to the foundation and subsequent powers of the Charity Organization Society (COS). The extent of unregulated private charity in the cities was seen as in itself a demoralizing force, and the COS was set up to try to bring to the administration of private charity the same spirit and some of the same rules as informed the administration of the Poor Law.

In the years between the two World Wars some of this insistence on the control of what we would now call 'the scrounger' began to weaken. The depth of the economic depression made it quite clear that the link between unemployment and character would be difficult to sustain, with whole villages put out of work. Even the COS had to admit that many unemployed people were in that condition solely because of the conditions of trade. The aim of the Welfare State legislation which followed the Second World War was that all citizens should be in receipt of a 'national minimum' which covered subsistence and a small amount more for some meagre participation in ordinary social living. The form and even the extent of provision may have changed with the introduction of the Welfare

State; but the discourse remains the same. The world was still seen as made up of individuals who need motivating to work, and the fear is still present that 'something for nothing' will destroy that motivation.

In the 1980s much of the old discourse and many of the old fears re-appeared in explicit form in the rhetoric of politicians and the require-ments of their administrators. The Department responsible for admin-istering 'relief' and 'insurance', for example, wrote of the former in 1985:

> While it is one of the functions of the social security system to help those who are unemployed, it is self-defeating if it creates barriers to the creation of jobs, to job mobility or to people rejoining the labour force. Clearly such obstacles exist if people believe themselves better off out of work than in work.
>
> (DHSS, 1985, quoted in Wilson, 1988)

The same concerns were expressed in 1834 about the Poor Law of 1601, and the passage expresses clearly the logic of 'less eligibility' that was formulated then. Indeed, the concept of the undeserving poor has re-appeared, those who voluntarily put themselves in a disadvantaged position in order to be eligible for state support.

The origins of 'casework' lie in the policing of charitable support, and the main function of the COS caseworker was to ensure that such support was not wasted. In the process he or she was called on to monitor the life-style of the person or family in receipt of support and to suggest better ways of managing money. In Victorian eyes this would probably entail monitoring attitudes and motivations — advising on better approaches to the world of work and ensuring that 'habits of industry' were built up and maintained. Men were encouraged into the discipline of productive work, and women into the discipline of good housekeeping and good mothering. (Because progress was monitored by *home* visiting, this process tended to bear down more heavily on women than on men.)

Such moral monitoring began to be seen as a skill in its own right, and the caseworkers — later 'social workers' — began to take their claims to professionalism from the exercise of this skill. The growing discipline of psychology provided a theoretical base for its exercise and developed techniques which could be taught and learned; in so doing it legitimated the profession and extended its own status as legitimate and relevant. As the techniques became psychologized, however, so did the content of case-work, and this aspect of social work came to be seen less as moral monitoring than as helping clients to survive in a social world which they found difficult. Moral monitoring has returned to some small extent dur-ing the last decade, with the 'casework' assessment of those in receipt of state benefits, but it is noticeable that this kind of work has not devolved onto social workers — whose professional stance has now changed to the extent that they would find it inappropriate — but to civil servants employed by the Department of Social Security.

Before the middle of the nineteenth century, the punishment of crime tended towards brutal measures aimed at deterring other potential offenders. During the century, however, a marked change took place in penal policy which had the effect of 'psychologizing' the penal system and bringing it into line with the belief, outside, in the reformability of the workshy and indigent. The essence of this change was that the offender is considered not just a showpiece from whose fate people may learn, but as a psychological subject reformable in his or her own right. A major intent is to change individuals — to terrify them and thus deter them from future offending, certainly, but increasingly also to resocialize them and give them what they are lacking to become productive workers. In sentencing, the questions are no longer just whether the offender broke the law and what the penalty shall be. Increasingly the courts are asking themselves *how* the law was broken, what the offence tells us about the offender, what can be added by enquiry into home circumstances or mental state. In other words, they begin to treat the evidence before them as symptoms on which a diagnostic decision is to be made — a decision about what sentence is most likely to have a reformative effect. Judgements are made by reference to a set of norms about how the 'ordinary person' would behave and therefore the direction and extremity of the offender's deviance from these norms. The offender is conceived as a defective but in principle perfectible mechanism. This is precisely the territory that I have described above as having been staked out by individual psychology and psychiatry — the assessment of norms and deviations, and the regulation of the deviant — and both disciplines soon become involved in the court process.

The three major elements of the regime within prisons in the nineteenth century were terror, discipline and labour. Prisoners were confined under a regime of 'even less eligibility' compared with people outside, and life was made uncomfortable and frightening for them. Work was required of all prisoners, and it was conducted in the sort of regimented way that was the dream of many factory owners and the norm of many schools. Whether the work was usefully productive or merely labour for the sake of it, prisoners were thought to learn 'habits of industry'; if it could be made productive it also helped cover the costs of imprisonment (and potentially kept wages down outside).

The aims of prison went beyond behavioural training and deterrence, however, even in the nineteenth century. Prison was also intended to work on the mind — to give criminals an opportunity for forced reflection on their lives and the circumstances of their offences, for them to repent and determine to reform. Religious advice was available in prisons from their early years. Charitable men and women of the middle classes visited prisoners to talk to them and reform by conversation and example. As we move into the twentieth century we find welfare/probation officers helping with resettlement and advising on how life should be run industriously and honestly, and education for prisoners begins to be provided. And, of course, psychologists were installed in the prisons, partly to help classify offenders, fit them to particular roles in the regime and predict their behaviour, but also with great licence to run treatment programmes from a wide variety of theoretical perspectives.

Such rehabilitative ideals reached their peak in the 1960s and early 1970s. Since then there has been a drift in official thinking away from the idea that prison might be used to reform criminals and towards seeing it as primarily concerned with their incarceration. Indeed, new discourses have been emerging in the criminal justice system as a whole and among academics and reformers. A reconceptualization of the 'subjects' of criminal justice may be in progress, away from psychological entities to be reformed and more towards relatively powerless people in need of protection from the state's potential excesses. (There is little evidence as yet that this discourse has influenced people's thinking outside academic and professional circles.)

Although reform is no longer advanced as prison's main purpose, the rhetoric of rehabilitation persists and continues to inform and colour practice. 'Humane containment' — providing opportunities for training and self-improvement while inside — is a declared goal. Prisoners serving more than very short terms are seen as having 'careers' in prison — time spans to be planned for and used to advantage — and both academics and prison officials advocate that these careers should be planned to make the best use of the available time (see for example, Mott, 1985 — particularly p.14). Prison psychologists and prison social workers continue to offer active programmes of treatment and counselling, and there have been moves to involve prison officers in their application. Productive work continues to be advocated for all prisoners. Thus the rhetoric of reform may be temporarily in abeyance, but prisoners are nonetheless conceived as 'psychological subjects', changeable by the right experience or at least open to learn from a carefully managed environment.

3   SOCIAL WORK IN THE COMMUNITY

This section of the chapter looks at 'supervision in the community' — mostly the work and powers of social workers. By 'supervision in the community' I mean not just, or even mainly, the formal duties of the probation and aftercare officer or of the social worker with respect to young people, but a range of ways in which social work and allied trades continue to 'manage the poor' on behalf of the state and society. We shall be looking particularly at how psychology has provided a knowledge-base and a legitimation for this management and itself gained legitimacy as a result.

Social work, like health visiting, rises from a number of different though related sources in the second half of the nineteenth century. One is the Charities Organization Society, which we have examined already. Others are the English and Scottish Societies for the Prevention of Cruelty to Children, established at around the same time. Hospital almoners are another source — originally employed to determine which patients of charity-supported hospitals could afford to pay, but developing into a counselling and social aid service. 'Moral welfare officers', funded at first on a voluntary basis by the Church and dealing with children living in circumstances which might be seen as presenting moral danger, are another source. By the end of the First World War there were also a substantial number of welfare workers attached to factories — particularly factories employing women in large numbers. 'Childcare officers' were employed to visit homes by a variety of state and voluntary bodies and for a variety of reasons. Probation work developed out of the police court missionaries of the nineteenth century, who were funded by proselytizing organizations such as the Church of England Temperance Society and the General Temperance Union of Scotland, and from the work of Discharged Prisoners' Aid Societies.

The original 'targets' of community supervisory and advisory work were equally heterogeneous. Different kinds of worker dealt with one or more of a wide range of 'problem groups': the sick, the old, the poor, the criminal, children in poverty, children in moral or physical danger, children truanting from school, orphans, women workers, discharged prisoners... What linked the different kinds of worker and their targets into effectively one kind of professional work was the practice of home visiting. The target area of social work epitomizes and collects together virtually all the 'problem categories' we have discussed in this chapter — the poor, the sick, children, and the products of the courts. Its early focus was the 'dangerous' classes whose conditions or habits might contaminate the population — those (the majority) not gathered together in prisons or workhouses or asylums — and the nation's children who were in danger. These became gradually reconceptualized as those in need and/or the socially incompetent, but the same kinds of people are involved.

The aim was not charitable support *per se* but normalization — returning the derelict to the fold. The notion was (and to an extent still is) that at least some of the clients could become normal, respectable citizens and support and regulate themselves without outside monitoring, if given the right guidance and support at a crucial point in their downward career. Social workers thus became one set of what Foucault calls 'the judges of normality':

> The judges of normality are present everywhere. We are in the society of the teacher-judge, the doctor-judge, the educator-judge, the 'social-worker'-judge; it is on them that the universal reign of the normative is based; and each individual, wherever he may find himself, subjects to it his body, his gestures, his behaviour, his aptitudes, his achievements.
>
> (Foucault, 1975, p. 304)

The method of 'treatment' was casework — 'diagnosis', 'treatment' and monitoring of this treatment's effects, on a case-by-case basis. Under the COS the 'treatment' was largely economic (advice and perhaps money), and the 'diagnosis' was to determine whether the case was 'deserving'. This 'financial' strand remains in modern social work: social work has kept its expertise in financial and budgeting matters via the ability to advise clients of what is available to them and to help navigate the shoals of heterogeneous and contradictory welfare provision. (The financial help has been restricted to advice in the more recent period; social workers have had few or no resources with which actually to *provide* aid.) In later years, with the growing influence of psychology over the profession of social work (see below), the element of financial aid and advice on resource management and the benefits available tended more and more to be seen as something separate from the empathic, psychological counselling by which the social worker tried to effect a lasting change in the client or family. It was the same workers who had both roles to carry out, however. In the modern more unified social services it may indeed be the same worker who is charged with the alleviation of poverty by advising the family on how to budget and 'work' the benefits system, and with inspecting the children for signs of mistreatment. The double role of advisor and monitor can sometimes make it difficult for the social worker to be clear about his or her perspective on a given family.

The casework approach tended very much to identify 'the family' as the appropriate site of intervention. Just as Jean Orr (1986) charges health visiting with reinforcing a particular view of 'the family' and how people should live — a particular set of power relations between the genders — so the same charge has been levelled against social work. The 'modern family' at whose development we looked briefly in an earlier section — father in paid employment, mother for preference a full-time housewife, and dependent children cared for at home — was urged on clients by Victorian visitors as a norm to which they should conform, a moral duty but also an economic regulator. To some extent this is still the case. It has led to problems for the social workers in certain cases, for this modern family was and is characterized as a private area immune to interference and subject to the will of the patriarchal husband, but at the same time some of the intervention is specifically to protect the children from the actions of this patriarch. Similarly, the Victorian ideal has the woman, the wife and mother, as the moral guide of the household, but some visitors will be inspecting the children for signs of the mother's neglect.

The other thing which is reinforced by the 'home visiting' style of social welfare and surveillance is the notion that problems are located at the level of individuals/families and can be treated at that level. As we have pointed out elsewhere of health visitors:

> ...they act to some extent as agents of social control, reinforcing societal norms and disseminating individualistic explanations for social problems. This is the case even if they themselves recognize the social/economic causes of these problems, because of the individualistic mode of their interaction.

(Abbot and Sapsford, 1990, p. 148)

The same can be said of social work. A modern generation of social workers is likely to identify the root cause and the ultimate cure of many of the problems which they encounter as aspects of social structures and processes which cannot be located or tackled at the level of individuals. Because their work lies with individuals/families, however, and they meet very real pain, distress and incompetence for which they have to find immediate alleviation, much of their work is necessarily individualistic. The client, on the other hand, does not see the broader explanations but merely the individualist interventions, and experience of these reinforces individualistic explanations in the clients' minds. The work with individual persons/families 'psychologizes' them — it helps them to see their problems and solutions as located within themselves and their immediate circumstances. At the same time the 'psychological complex' works to reinforce casework as an appropriate way of working; it helps to make it natural to see problems as located in or associated with the 'cases' which are individual persons or families.

An important stage in the psychologization of casework and of the social work profession was the increased specialization of sub-branches during the course of the twentieth century, each of which accumulated its own knowledge-base seen as relevant to its work and a justification of its working practices. When many of these specialities were again brought together into a generic service, the superficially different but essentially congruent knowledge-bases formed a fusion in which each reinforced the others' validity.

Working with the greater confidence of a substantial history of practice, social work would now see itself as a distinctive area of expertise with its own knowledge-base separate from those of sociology or psychology. Nonetheless, textbooks continue to direct students' attention to the value of psychological theories and techniques, explicitly or implicitly. Psychology may not be seen as the total of the social workers' repertoire of techniques, but its relevance to casework is 'obvious' to social work trainers. For example, one textbook declares in its introduction:

> We make considerable use of concepts and methods derived from behavioural psychology, but by no means...do we see social workers as second-rate psychologists. There can be no doubt that social work is now a professional activity in its own right, drawing on several academic disciplines but having also its own body of specialized skills and knowledge.
>
> (Collins and Collins, 1981, pp. 2–3)

As the book goes on, however, it is organized as a psychologist would organize it, with chapters on various individual 'treatments' and a final one on working with groups. Another textbook makes a stronger case for the separateness of social work, but also stresses the importance of theory as underlying practice — and the preferred theories are psychological:

> My view is that knowledge derived from medicine, law, philosophy
> and the social sciences will aid your assessment, but if you are intent
> on finding a 'true' explanation...you will remain confused and disil-
> lusioned. Psychology has been more useful in the degree to which
> you can apply some of the theories...if you are prepared to see theor-
> etical contributions as ways of enriching your thinking and under-
> standing, you will gain a broad framework of information through
> which you will recognize the complexities and possible causes of
> human suffering.
>
> (Coulshead, 1988, p. 6)

In other words, social work has its own distinctive expertise, but it is an
expertise of practice and the experience of successful practice. Without
underlying theoretical perspectives the practitioner is working in the
dark, and it is psychology that most usefully provides such perspectives.
(Note also that the target is identified as 'human suffering' — a very
psychological way of framing the problem.)

One interesting aspect of this psychologization is that when problems
become attributed to the mind rather than the station of the client they
largely appear to lose their character as class based. This means that a
part of the ideology which social work's practice tends to reinforce — an
integral part of the discourse of individualism — is that problems are
specific to persons and circumstances, and not an aspect of class position:

> Psychology provides a scientific, rather than a moral, language for
> talking about these social problems, and in the process these prob-
> lems *lost their 'class character'*. Where in the nineteenth century 'the
> Social Problem' referred to the whole of the lower classes, by the
> interwar years we have multiple social problems, scientifically
> identified...
>
> (Clarke, 1988, p.35)

Another part is its empowerment of the expert by devaluation of the
clients' accounts of their problems. Psychology is very much an interpret-
ative science, treating what is said less as factual information than as
symptoms to be interpreted in terms of underlying theory. The psychologist, to the extent that his or her claim to have a broader and better
founded understanding of human behaviour and motives than the laity is
accepted, acquires the power to tell the client what his or her life and
problems are 'really' like and therefore what he or she should do about
them. This same power is acquired by the 'psychologically validated'
social worker.

Thus we have briefly traced the growth of particular branches of psychology — the 'individual psychology' of psychometric measurement and
the assessment of personality and ability, the models of behaviour orig-
inating in Freudian psychology and developed and changed by a variety of
successors, and the psychological techniques of interviewing and counselling — in the handling of youth, the poor and the criminal. Various

psychologists have held a variety of positions on areas of psychological debate such as whether traits are innate or learned and the extent to which it is helpful to see individuals as in control of their actions. The debates take place within a single amorphous but essentially unified form of discourse, however one which declares the individual to be the locus of explanations and the target of intervention.

4   CONCLUSIONS

In this chapter we have traced a mode of social intervention through a wide range of social institutions. Children are targeted at school, prisoners in the prison and other offenders in the community, together with the poor, the elderly, the unemployed, the mentally ill and other 'problem groups'. What makes some of these groups a problem and others a target to be monitored to prevent problems is the concept that all citizens should follow the path laid out for them, of self-reliance and individual competition for reward by means of the paid work that is available to them; this is what is seen as keeping the society orderly, efficient and integral. These values were explicit in the Victorian era and became more implicit in the 1960s and 1970s, but they persisted despite the lack of emphasis, and they rose again to some extent in the political rhetoric of the 1980s.

The family has been a particular target of social intervention since the nineteenth century, and within the family the mother has been particularly targeted. 'Visitors' of various kinds, backed by first medical and then psychological experts, have worked with a succession of theories about how mothers influence their children — targeting first the question of physical and moral health, but moving eventually on to the question of the child's sanity and adjustment. They have monitored the performance of the working-class mother in her duty of rearing the nation's children and offered advice or taken more punitive sanctions where she appeared not to be carrying out the job satisfactorily. In later years, since the Second World War in particular, the same scrutiny and the same theories have been brought to bear on the middle-class mother as well.

In the process these 'visitors' — health visitors, social workers, child care officers, welfare officers and the like — have helped to maintain and strengthen a view of what 'the family' should be — of how men, women and children should organize their lives with respect to one another. We may note that the maintenance of the family stereotype has done women little service, given the manifest inequalities of power and often of material resource concealed within the privacy of the stereotype nuclear family. The approach is also to a large extent 'colour-blind'; it fails to acknowledge in more than an academic way the variety of domestic forms which different minority groups have imported from their previous cultures or invented in response to current problems, and it assumes one model of child development as good for all the different possible ways of bringing up a child. The overall aim is 'normalization' — determining the proper way to organize a family and bring up children, and using this as a criterion for making judgements about the diversity which it actually encounters. In the earlier years of the period we have been discussing, the intention to normalize was vocal and explicit. In later years some workers have denied having such an intention, but normalization nonetheless tends to underlie their practice. While individual workers may be aware of the range of domestic arrangements to be found in Britain and wary, from their sociological training, of privileging one form over any other, nonetheless their attempts to keep conventional nuclear families intact and the creation of variant forms (such as one-parent families) as special targets of attention will reinforce the image of the ideologically correct family form as 'normal' in their clients' eyes. Indeed, the legislation within which they work often forces them in this direction.

The psychologies which have been seen in this chapter as informing this kind of practice and as supported and reinforced by it have tended to 'normalize' and 'psychologize' individuals and their situations in two over-lapping ways. Their original point of application was 'the deviant' — mentally subnormal children and adults, malfunctioning families, delin-quents, criminals — and they offered a way of trying to return these deviants to normality, or else of declaring them untreatable and to be segregated. (These may be opposing strategies, but the same *discourse* informs both; in both, the problem is formulated in very similar terms, and the solutions have very similar targets.) In defining what 'the deviant' was deviant *from*, however, these psychologies very quickly come to define the social world in terms of dimensions on which individuals are treated and strategies for their management. In this way the whole popu-lation, as individuals, become the subjects of psychology.

We have traced, briefly and crudely, the history of some of the professions which have grown out of the 'visiting movement' to offer advice and aid to families. As professions they have a somewhat ambivalent status still. Doctors, engineers, physicists and others of unquestionable status share a degree of autonomy in their professional work because of their privi-leged access to an acknowledged knowledge-base. Health visitors and social workers, despite their aspiration to a professional knowledge-base and their extensive use of psychology to provide one, are responsible to the state (or in some current cases and more earlier ones to charitable bodies which function in the way we would now expect the state to func-tion). They may act within their own area of autonomy — which is mostly the contents of casework practice with individual clients — but most of their more strategic or 'structural' decisions have to be validated by some other agency or body.

People in the 'helping professions' would often regard their first concern as being the interests of the client, in the same way that a doctor might regard his or her first concern as being the alleviating of the patient's condition. This is one thing that 'being professional' means. The problem, for any profession which uses psychology, is *which* needs of the client are to be served — those which the client announces, or those which the professional ascribes? This will be a particular problem where the client is not a volunteer but someone referred by the courts or the police, or accepting supervision as a condition of release from prison or hospital, or in order to avoid an unwanted consequence such as the removal of a child from the home, or in order to obtain financial resources — the list of possible qualifying conditions is so long that it is not clear what kind of person might qualify clearly as having voluntarily asked for social work. (In the world of health visiting no client is ever a volunteer, in the sense that health visitors go to every home with a child, not waiting to be called in.) Further, 'being professional' also entails acting 'responsibly' — bearing the needs of the wider society in mind. And again, one may validly ask *which* needs, and who is to determine that they are needs?

The third trend at which we have looked is the development of psychology itself — the individual psychology which classifies and normalizes, and the analytic psychology which looks for internal (generally childhood) explanations for current deviation from the norm. If we had looked elsewhere, at the world of industrial employment, we should have been looking at 'group' and 'interactional' psychology as well as psychometrics, but a very similar story could be told (see for example Hollway, 1991). These psychologies have developed during this same period, as a result of the way that society and its problems are conceptualized, but also contributing as a causal agent to that conceptualization. Different psychologies have grown up in different parts of the social field, and in their detail they may be fundamentally opposed to each other. They share, however, a set of views about what sort of a society we live in and how it is best managed: they all tend to share a view of society as a machine which is improvable. What psychology contributes to social work, health visiting, etc., over and above a knowledge-base and a validation of practice, is a long-term view of a society which can be rationally managed through the rational management of individuals — a Fabian utopia, in essence.

The 'psychology' discussed here forms only a part of the full range of what is contained within social psychology, therapy and counselling. To cover this range in detail would be beyond the scope of this chapter. We might fruitfully note, however, two kinds of psychology which can often lie outside the boundaries: recent sociologically informed work and work influenced by ideas of discourse — for example the Foucault-influenced work of Henriques et al. (1984), or analyses of the construction and reproduction of ideology in everyday life such as the work of Michael Billig and his colleagues (1988), or the discourse analysis of Potter and Wetherell (1987) or the radical reconstruction attempted by Rom Harré (1984); secondly, the systems theory which informs both family therapy and various kinds of network analysis (see for example Dallos, 1991) and which attempts to look at the symbolic interactions of co-resident or co-working people at a level which is not reducible to the intentions of any one of them.

Both lie outside the discourse because, and to the extent that, they try to represent social reality at something other than the level of individuals. They also lie outside it because they are not primarily concerned with the causes of behaviour, in the linear sense of the term 'cause'. They are not concerned with the antecedents of particular actions, but with states or styles of life and how meanings are manipulated to maintain them. They are different psychologies in the very real sense that they accept neither the problems and goals of the 'psychology' which we have been discussing nor the overall world-view which underlies it. Systems theory, indeed, has been taken up in social work practice and has had some 'de-individu-alizing' impact on it. This impact should not be exaggerated, however; while systems theory impacts on social work, the casework situation has an impact on systemic practice.

A final point to note is that any science contributes to the managers and monitors of society one very substantial benefit — that it diverts a pro-portion of the problematic issues out of the arena of debate. By accepting that certain kinds of issues are amenable to scientific solution — 'matters of fact' — we empower experts both to act on our behalf and ultimately to determine what our 'best interests' are. A part of the control which this establishment of expertise exerts is achieved

> by taking what is essentially a political problem, removing it from the realm of political discourse, and recasting it in the neutral lan-guage of science. Once this is accomplished the problems have become technical ones.
>
> (Foucault, 1982, p. 196)

REFERENCES

Abbot, P. and Sapsford, R. (1990) 'Health visiting: policing the family' in Abbot, P. and Wallace, C. (eds) *The Sociology of the Caring Professions*, Basingstoke, Falmer.

Billig, M., Condor, S., Edwards, D., Gane, M., Middleton, D. and Radley, A. (1988) *Ideological Dilemmas: A Social Psychology of Everyday Thinking*, London, Sage.

Board of Control (1934) *Report of the Departmental Committee on Sterilization*, Cmnd 4485, London, HMSO.

Brown, J.A.C. (1954) *The Social Psychology of Industry*, Harmondsworth, Penguin.

Burt, C. (1925) *The Young Delinquent*, London, University of London Press.

Clarke, J. (1988) Unit 13 'Social work: the personal and the political' in D211 *Social Problems and Social Welfare*, Milton Keynes, The Open University.

Collins, J. and Collins, M. (1981) *Achieving Change in Social Work*, London, Heinemann.

Coulshead, V. (1988) *Social Work Practice: an Introduction*, London, Macmillan.

Coulshead, V. (1991) *Social Work Practice: an Introduction*, 2nd edition, London, Macmillan.

Dallos, R. (1991) *Family Belief Systems, Therapy and Change*, Buckingham, The Open University Press.

Foucault, M. (1979) 'On governmentality', *Ideology and Consciousness*, vol.6, pp.5–21.

Foucault, M. (1982) 'The subject and power' in Dreyfus, H. and Rabinow, P. (eds) *Michel Foucault: Beyond Structuralism and Hermeneutics*, Brighton, Harvester.

Galton, F. (1883) *Inquiries into Human Faculty and its Development*, London, Macmillan.

Harré, R. (1984) *Personal Being: a Theory for Individual Psychology*, Oxford, Blackwell.

Henriques, J., Hollway, W., Urwin, C., Venn, C. and Walkerdine, V. (1984) *Changing the Subject: Psychology, Social Regulation and Subjectivity*, London, Methuen.

Hollway, W. (1991) *Work Psychology and Organizational Behaviour: Managing the Individual at Work*, London, Sage.

Jameson Report (1956) *An Enquiry into Health Visiting*, London, HMSO.

Maudsley, H. (1874) *Responsibility in Mental Disease*, London, King.

Mott, J. (1985) *Adult Prisons and Prisoners in England and Wales 1970–1982: a Review of the Findings of Social Research*, Home Office Research Study No.84, London, HMSO.

Orr, J. (1986) 'Feminism and health visiting' in Webb, C. (ed) *Feminist Practice in Women's Health Care*, Chichester, Wiley.

Pearson, K. (1904) 'On the laws of inheritance in man', *Biometrika*, vol.3, pp.131–90.

Poor Law Commission (1834) *Report from His Majesty's Commissioners for Inquiry into the Administration and Practical Operation of the Poor Laws*, London, HMSO.

Potter, J. and Wetherell, M. (1987) *Discourse and Social Psychology: Beyond Attitudes and Behaviour*, London, Sage.

Rose, N. (1985) *The Psychological Complex: Psychology, Politics and Society in England 1869–1939*, London, Routledge and Kegan Paul.

Rose, N. (1989) 'Individualizing psychology' in Shotter, J. and Gergen, K.J. (eds) *Texts of Identity*, London, Sage.

Summer, B. (1981) *Working with People: an Introduction to the Caring Professions*, London, Cassell.

Wilson, M. (1988) Unit 22 'The welfare state in crisis' in D211 *Social Problems and Social Welfare*, Milton Keynes, The Open University.

STUDY QUESTIONS

1   What are the main features of the Psychological Complex? That is, what are the core, continuing features rather than those which may change over time?

2   What are the assumptions in the Psychological Complex about the nature of individuals and about the best ways to manage social order?

3   What are the likely social consequences of dividing the population into 'normal' and 'deviant' individuals?

4   What are the advantages and disadvantages, and for whom, of the growth of the Pyschological Complex?

5   In what ways was the Psychological Complex significant for the development of social work? What features are particularly emphasized in social work by comparison with other social institutions?

CHAPTER 3
THE RISE AND FALL OF SOCIAL WORK

MARY LANGAN

> During the last twenty years, whenever the British people have identified and investigated a social problem, there has followed a national call for more social work and more trained social workers.
>
> (Titmuss, 1965, p. 85)

In Chapter 1 we noted the twentieth century trend for caring functions to be undertaken by 'strangers', by members of the 'caring professions'. In the 1960s, social work came of age as social workers sought to secure their place alongside established professionals working within the framework of the welfare state, such as nurses, teachers and doctors. An influential lobby, ably represented by Richard Titmuss, Britain's leading post-war social policy academic, pressed the social work cause. Titmuss' account of the growing demand for social work and social workers reflected the rising ambitions of the new profession.

The Committee on Local Authority and Allied Personal Social Services, established in 1965 with Sir Frederic (later Lord) Seebohm in the chair, fully vindicated the aspirations of Titmuss and the wider world of social work. The committee's report, published in 1968, endorsed the fusion of diverse social work tasks into the role of the generic social worker, and recommended the establishment of local authority social services departments to coordinate and supervise the provision of social support. Writing in a special issue of the journal *Social Work* in October 1968, David Donnison, then Professor of Social Administration at London University, described the Seebohm Report as 'a great state paper' while an editorial in the same issue declared that 'for many social workers' it represented 'the fulfilment of their highest hopes' (quoted in Sinfield, 1970, p. 24).

The Seebohm Report reflected the commitment of 1960s social democracy to tackling the problems of society through state intervention guided by experts with appropriate scientific and technical skills. It was also imbued with an older liberal commitment to enhancing social citizenship through promoting greater equality and solidarity. For its authors, the new social services departments were not to be restricted to piecemeal social engineering, nor were they to be limited to dealing with problems of personal incapacity, whether physical, mental or social. Their brief was to 'reach far beyond the discovery and rescue of social casualties' to 'enable the greatest possible number of individuals to act reciprocally, giving and receiving service for the well-being of the whole community' (Seebohm, 1968, para. 2). Seebohm envisaged a progressive universalistic service transcending the stigmatizing and paternalistic traditions of local authority and voluntary welfare agencies. For its more enthusiastic supporters, the 'fifth social service' aimed to complement the achievements of the post-war welfare reforms (education, health, housing and social security) by redressing residual social inequalities and thereby promoting a deeper sense of mutuality and community.

But, as we shall see, Seebohm was a false dawn for social work. The new era of social service expansion and professional advance for social work turned out to be short-lived. Scarcely had the unifying dynamic of the 1960s ushered in the generic social worker and the social services department, than the forces of fragmentation were unleashed by the combination of economic recession and political retrenchment in the 1970s. In retrospect, Seebohm marked the high tide of social work, the peak of a wave of political and professional optimism that slowly ebbed away over the next decade:

> The Seebohm Report can best be understood and appreciated as the product of a watershed: as the beginning of a period of doubt and austerity to be followed by outright disbelief in the enlarged role of the state to which the post-war years had given effect...in the optimism of the 1960s there were the seeds of a less rosy, even despairing period for social policy.
>
> (Webb and Wistow, 1987, p. 54)

While the next two chapters look at the multiplicity of challenges that pushed social work to the brink of despair in the 1980s, here we look more closely at the moment of Seebohm and at how the high hopes it expressed gradually evaporated in the succeeding decade.

I THE HIGH TIDE OF SOCIAL WORK

The demand for a reappraisal of social welfare services in the mid-1960s, which led to the establishment of the Seebohm Committee, was the result of a number of factors (Hall, 1976, p. 17). The fragmented character of local authority welfare provision, the legacy of the post-war structure discussed in Chapter 1, had long been the target of criticism. Children's departments were responsible for children and families; welfare departments looked after older people, people with disabilities and the homeless; health departments were concerned with people with mental illness and learning difficulties.

In the late 1950s, both the Ingleby Report on children and young people and the Younghusband Report on social work in health and welfare departments emphasized the need for better coordinated services. Other critics noted wide variations in the range and quality of services and inflexibility in responding to changing needs and demands. Changing definitions of social needs, particularly in relation to juvenile delinquency, were also influential. A series of reports, culminating in Lord Longford's 1965 White Paper, *The Child, the Family and the Young Offender*, emphasized the role of social factors in the causation of crime and promoted the role of some sort of community-based 'family service' in both preventing delinquency and in rehabilitating offenders (Clarke, 1980).

The social work lobby, which was formally organized as a 'working group' including Titmuss and other prominent academics and senior social work figures, opposed a narrowly defined family service based on the existing children's departments. They campaigned in favour of a wider conception of social work, embracing also the functions of the health and welfare departments, and aspects of the work of the education and housing departments, though excluding probation and social security. Key figures in the social policy working group, R. Huws Jones, Principal of the National Institute for Social Work Training, and J. N. Morris, Professor of Social Medicine at London University, subsequently became members of the Seebohm Committee (Hall, 1976, p. 23). Though there was some criticism of the lack of field-level social workers (and the paucity of medical representation) on the Seebohm Committee, the more telling criticism was of the preponderance of senior figures from the social work establishment. In the view of one observer, this could only 'heighten anxiety that a major function of the report has been to strengthen the position of the profession and of its administrators' (Sinfield, 1970, p. 41).

The Seebohm Report proposed bringing the diverse local authority welfare services together within a new social services department, which would thus become a major force within local government. A unified, centralized social services department, complete with local area teams and controlled through a local government inspectorate would provide the institutional foundation for a greatly enhanced role for the emerging social work profession. In Scotland, the Kilbrandon Committee (1961–64), formed more specifically in response to concerns about juvenile delinquency, proposed a similar set of reforms, leading to the establishment of social work departments.

The Seebohm Report took an essentially optimistic view of social problems in contemporary Britain. It considered that conditions of post-war economic expansion sustained by political consensus and a comprehensive welfare state had largely eradicated the major structural problems of poverty, ignorance, disease, slum housing and mass unemployment, the 'five giants' identified in Beveridge's famous wartime report. Now that the problems that had so preoccupied earlier generations of social reformers had been vanquished, what remained were a relatively small number of people who, because of diverse personal problems, experienced difficulties in adjusting to the complexities of life in modern society. Such people ranged from parents who, through ignorance or incompetence, were bringing up their children inadequately, to those who lacked the social competence or support to find their way through the complex networks of the welfare system, or who simply lacked social support in times of crisis, or were in need through age or disability.

A similar spirit imbued parallel social legislation, notably the 1969 Children and Young Persons Act and the 1970 Chronically Sick and Disabled Persons Act. The 1969 Act reflected a shift away from the traditional preoccupation with the link between crime and punishment towards a more social democratic emphasis on prevention and rehabilitation. It sought to reduce the role of the courts, the police and custodial institutions and expand that of social services departments and social workers, working with young offenders and their families in the community. The 1970 Act also expanded the role of local authorities, giving them the responsibility of identifying the needs of people with disabilities and providing appropriate services. Although both acts were controversial and neither was fully implemented, they exerted considerable influence on the organization and practice of social work in the 1970s.

The separation of personal problems from issues of material inequality provided the opening within which social work could establish its particular professional claims. As we have seen in Chapter 2, the knowledge-base of social work lay in the field of human functioning and interaction; its skills were those of providing advice and support to help individuals (and their families) to function more effectively. From this perspective what was required was not specialized workers from a variety of agencies dealing with different client groups, but a generic worker capable of grasping the variety of human experiences, assessing individual and family needs and offering services to meet them. The modern social worker came into existence as an amalgam of half a dozen or more occupational groups — psychiatric and medical social workers, and 'officers' concerned with offenders, children, mental health, housing and educational welfare.

The creation of a common career structure and training curriculum aimed to foster professional competence and coherence. Although the first 'generic' social work course was launched at the London School of Economics in 1954, it took another twenty years before professional qualifications in social work became properly established. In 1959 the Younghusband Report recommended training outside the universities from which the existing social work elite had emerged. In 1962 the Council for Training in Social Work authorized a Certificate in Social Work to be awarded on the successful completion of a two-year course, usually at a polytechnic or college of further education. Most students were seconded on grants from local authorities for which they had been working as unqualified social workers. As a result of the impetus provided by Seebohm and the new social services departments, as well as pressure from the newly unified professional body, the British Association of Social Workers, the Central Council for Education and Training in Social Work was established in 1971. It rationalized curricula and supervised courses, introducing the Certificate of Qualification in Social Work in 1971, the first universally recognized professional qualification in social work in Britain. This structure of professional training embodied the commitment to 'generic' social work and provided a powerful impetus to its development as the dominant approach to the provision of personal social services.

However, there was a contradiction at the heart of the Seebohm Report which was carried over into the subsequent debate about the scope of the personal social services in the 1970s. On the one hand, it proclaimed a universal approach, aiming to transcend the stigmatizing selective approach of much of the existing welfare services. On the other hand, the individualistic character of social work intervention and the continuing preoccupation of the social services with 'problem families' and 'difficult personalities' meant that, in practice, social work retained its focus on a particular section of the community. The lack of any major expansion of social services funding meant that the new departments could never escape the selectivist legacy of the Poor Law.

The universalist theme of the Seebohm Report was evident in its recommendation that the new social services department should not be narrowly concerned with the problems of a targeted minority, but should take a wider responsibility for helping people to cope with difficulties, such as bereavement or child rearing, which are common to all families. The new department was to offer 'a door on which to knock' for all those in need of help, whether individuals or families, whether they required institutional care (in homes for children or older people), local facilities (day or family centres) or intensive personal support (casework). In addition, they would act as a personalized point of contact for those needing assistance in negotiating the complexities of the wider welfare system (especially housing and social security).

Contemporary criticisms of Seebohm reveal not only the early recognition of some of the weak points of the new conception of the social work project, but more significantly the prevailing sense of high expectations about what social work could achieve. This is particularly striking in the commentaries on the report from prominent figures in the Fabian Society, then acting as a radical think tank on the left flank of the Labour Party and with close links to the social work lobby. Though these commentators were broadly in sympathy with Seebohm, some were disappointed the report had not gone even further.

Thus, while noting the failure of the Government to allocate any additional expenditure to the new social services departments, Peter Townsend summed up 'the broad conclusion' of a special Fabian Society conference in February 1969: 'The Seebohm Report is constructive and its chief recommendation to merge the local services in one department is justified' (Townsend, 1970, p. 7). 'But', he continued, 'as an example of planning the report is lacking in analysis, drive and vision'. He considered that 'a great opportunity had been missed' to launch a 'major new family and community welfare service' with the aims of equalizing resources locally, reducing social isolation, increasing family support and enhancing 'community integration' (ibid., p. 22). Writing in similar terms in another Fabian collection, Muriel Brown appealed for a service that was 'comprehensive in provision, universal in scope', a service that had 'an obvious contribution to make to the entire population in, for example, improving social cohesion and promoting integration in meaningful communities' (Brown, 1972, p. 66).

In reality neither the Seebohm Report nor the social services departments that were established in 1970 could carry the weight of the Fabians' great schemes. Despite all the universalist rhetoric, social workers retained authoritarian statutory powers — in relation to children and people with mental illness — that gave them the right to knock on selected people's doors, rather than waiting benignly for clients to visit them. Lacking the resources from the outset to provide services according to need, social workers were obliged to remain parsimonious custodians of limited resources and selective benefactors of the modern equivalent of the deserving poor. Although it was relatively little acknowledged at the time, the other significant context for the practice of social work was the 'informal sector' — the work of primary carers in the family and community. The new departments did relatively little in practice to alleviate the burdens of female carers in the home. Indeed, such 'labours of love' formed part of the taken for granted assumptions of the emergent profession. At best, it seemed, the reponsibilities of social work extended to finding ways of aiding women to carry out such duties more effectively where either their skills or attitudes were found to be flawed.

Brown could boldly proclaim that 'equality can only thrive in a society that makes universal provision for social welfare, selecting and positively discriminating in favour of some categories of need or certain areas only on a basis of universal service' (Brown, 1972, p. 70). But Britain in the early 1970s was not about to become a more equal society and the social services departments were ill-equipped to withstand a growing current moving in the opposite direction. Later critics noted that, whatever the aspirations of the Fabians, the new social democracy was in practice concerned merely with 'identifying emergent problems as minor internal malfunctions of the system, requiring only further corrective technical strategies' (Clarke et al., 1980, p. 179). These authors noted that Seebohm offered a 'magical resolution' of social problems that were regarded as residual, but were in fact manifestations of 'the first rumblings of the economic crisis'. Their view that the task of the generic social worker was to fill the 'empty centre' of the social services department became, as we shall see, a central theme of the radical social work movement in the 1970s.

Whatever the deficiencies of the Seebohm Report itself, by the time it was implemented in the 1970 Local Authority Social Services Act, its radical edge had been considerably blunted. The housing and education aspects of welfare were excluded from the jurisdiction of the new social services departments and the emphasis on prevention had virtually disappeared. Furthermore there was to be no local government inspectorate, thus giving the Secretary of State more direct authority over the departments. When Labour lost office in the 1970 General Election the reforming impetus behind the new legislation was lost. The climate of stringency and reaction that lay ahead was inauspicious for the Seebohm Report's progressive features and for its fragile progeny — the social services departments and the social work profession.

2   THE REALITY GAP

Any intention there may have been at the time of the Seebohm Report of producing a universal service to set alongside the National Health Service has been destroyed by the twin forces of rising demand and public expenditure restraint which characterised the second half of the 1970s. Despite a few faltering steps towards a universal service, the personal social services have not fully escaped from the the residual model of their Poor Law origins.

(Webb, 1980, p. 279)

According to Webb, 'the first three years of the 1970s were the brief heyday of the reorganised personal social services' (ibid., p. 285). During this period the new social services departments were established around the country and the new social work profession expanded rapidly. The climate of growth and optimism allowed social workers to consolidate their position and a degree of consensus was preserved around the broad approach of the Seebohm Report. The pattern of growth is reflected in the expansion of those employed in personal social services. In 1954, there had been 3,000 field social workers in various agencies. By 1971, there were 10,346, while this number had more than doubled by 1976 to 21,182 (NALGO, 1989, p. 8). As Table 3.1 shows, field social work led this expansion but there were significant developments in other forms of social work employment.

Table 3.1   Personal social services workforce, 1971–1976

	1971	1976	% change per year
Social workers	10,346	21,182	20.8
Home helps	32,550	43,892	7.0
Staff in homes for elderly	37,684	49,970	6.6

Source: NALGO, 1989, p. 8, Table 3

In this climate of expansion, it was briefly possible for political and professional optimism about the future of personal social services to override doubts, concerns and conflicts. Potential conflicts between the bureaucratic and hierarchical structure of the new local authority departments and decentralized social work teams were largely contained. However, even in the early 1970s the progressive impact of the social policy reforms was already being curtailed by the new government. Thus key sections of the Children and Young Persons Act were never implemented: the age of criminal responsibility was not raised to fourteen, detention centres continued to be used for under-seventeens, and the imposition of custodial sentences increased (Pinker, 1982). In a similar way, the implementation of the Chronically Sick and Disabled Persons Act was piecemeal and delayed.

'By 1973,' writes Webb, 'the honeymoon was over', as, under central government pressure, local authorities executed 'a chaotic retreat from growth' (Webb, 1980, p. 286). Although spending on personal social services was relatively protected during this period and, indeed, continued to grow into the 1980s, the years of *rapid* expansion were brought to a halt. The result was that social services departments came up against budgetary limitations before the full range of their intended activities could be established. To make matters worse, changing social, economic and demographic patterns produced increasing demands for, and pressures on, social work. The same recessionary forces which dictated tighter controls on public spending created, for the first time in the post-war period, significant unemployment, growing poverty and deprivation. These factors, together with demographic trends which produced a simultaneous expansion in the numbers of both young and old people, as well as a growing number of lone parent families, combined to increase demand for social services support.

In December 1974 the Government issued a circular to social services departments urging them to 'concentrate their effort mainly on those in the most acute and immediate need: children at risk of ill-treatment, the very old and severely handicapped in urgent need of care and individuals and families at imminent risk of breakdown' (Smith, 1983, p. 22). Within six years of Seebohm the selective mentality of the old Poor Law had come to prevail over the universalist aspirations of the report's more radical proponents. As Table 3.2 indicates, the second half of the 1970s saw a very different pattern of spending on personal social services from that which accompanied the initial implementation of the Seebohm Report.

Table 3.2   Percentage growth per year in personal social services expenditure, 1970–1974 and 1975–79

	1970–74	1975–79
Current expenditure	16.5	3.1
Capital expenditure	11.95	-9.2
Total PSS expenditure	15.8	1.9

Source: NALGO, 1989, p. 9, Table 4

The retreat from Seebohm and the onset of austerity provoked a growing crisis of confidence among social workers. They were directly affected by public spending curbs, often at the same time as they were being given wider responsibilities under new legislation. Social workers were confronted with demands for material as well as personal assistance, which they could do little to satisfy, partly because of their professional orientation and lack of resources and partly because such support was supposed to come from other welfare services. In practice, social workers found themselves increasingly drawn into negotiations with social security offices, housing departments, electricity and gas boards, etc. in attempts to help their clients. Such negotiations put social workers in difficult positions. Were they acting as advocates for their clients or gatekeepers to public resources? Were they supposed to engage professionally with clients' emotional demands or try to help them satisfy their material needs?

Debates that had receded in the vigorous atmosphere of the early social services departments — about the relative merits of specialist and generic practice, about the tension between the caring and controlling functions of social work, about conflicts of loyalty between clients and society — now emerged again with renewed intensity.

3   PROFESSIONALISM IN QUESTION

Whereas in 1968 professionalism seemed about to triumph, today, despite the fact that social work has become established within the apparatus of the state on bureau-professional lines, there is a sense of retreat and even rejection of the professional ideal.

(Parry and Parry, 1979, p. 44)

According to Sinfield, the Seebohm Committee consisted essentially of the vested interests of the social work profession. Given that the views of the social work lobby so powerfully influenced the final report, he expressed concern that social workers were at risk of putting their professional interests before those of the public: 'a citizen reading the report might conclude that it had more to do with the work satisfaction and career structure of the professional social worker than it had to do with his own needs or rights in the modern welfare state' (Sinfield, 1970, p. 24). In the context of the wider difficulties facing social work in the 1970s such observations not only persisted but intensified, exacerbating the crisis of professional confidence.

In the short term, however, Seebohm and the subsequent legislation establishing local authority social services departments, together with the enactment of the new law concerning children, all enhanced the professional position and authority of social workers. The social worker aspired to a similar status to that enjoyed by the medical profession in the health service, and the new framework appeared to offer this. The Children and Young Persons Act, in particular, gave wide powers to social workers in the decision to bring a child to court, in the preparation of reports on the child and its family, and in the provision of 'treatment'. Under the terms of a care order committing a child to local authority care, the social worker acquired significant power over the child. In the field of mental health too, social workers acquired significant statutory powers, conferred under the 1959 Mental Health Act in relation to the compulsory admission of people considered to be suffering from mental illness to hospital.

Though social workers engaged in field work accounted for less than 15 per cent of the staff employed in the new social services departments, they acquired considerable prestige as the leading professional group. In fact the bulk of social services staff were engaged in residential care, in day care centres and community activities (such as 'meals on wheels' and home helps) as well as in administrative and clerical tasks. Yet field social workers were the public face of the social services department and the virtually exclusive focus of public discussion. One indication of the higher status of social work was the growing proportion of men entering the ranks of the profession (Walton, 1975; Brook and Davis, 1985). Although traditionally a predominantly female occupation, social work in the 1970s came to include more and more men, and they were soon disproportionately represented in the higher administrative grades.

As part of a wider trend of questioning the legitimacy of professional authority, social workers came under growing public scrutiny in the 1970s. The death of Maria Colwell in 1973, while formally under the care of East Sussex County Council, provoked the first major wave of public criticism of social workers. It was to be the first of many similar cases in which the professionalism of social work and the skill, training and competence of its practitioners were openly disparaged. Yet, while social workers were targeted for failing to intervene to prevent child abuse, they were also being accused of neglecting the rights of clients in their over-zealous exercise of their statutory powers — in relation both to people with mental illness and children.

Social workers were criticized for resorting excessively to compulsory admissions to mental hospitals (Bean, 1980). In 1979 the British Association of Social Workers proposed to the government body reviewing the operation of the Mental Health Act that social workers should have an independent role complementing that of doctors in compulsory admissions. This was rejected, on the grounds that it was 'an ill-considered attempt to enlarge the legal powers of social workers' (Bean, 1979, p. 105). In enforcing care orders on children, Parsloe observed that 'the discretion of the social worker in England is subject to few checks' (Parsloe, 1976, p. 79). In dealing with juvenile delinquents, Wilding considered that 'the social worker's all embracing role as diagnostician, prescriber, treatment executant, sanctioner in the case of non-compliance, and befriender also gives grounds for concern' (Wilding, 1982, p. 106). He argued that such a 'concentration of power and responsibility in one person is as unhealthy, and as considerable a threat to liberty, as is the failure to guarantee the separation of powers in the body politic' (ibid., p. 106). Wilding was roundly critical of the 'excessive claims and limited achievements' of the social work profession (ibid., p. 89).

Social work as a profession also came under pressure from the emerging managerial hierarchy in local government. The unification of the social work profession under the aegis of the local authority social services department forged what Henry Mintzberg has characterized as a 'professional bureaucracy' combining standardized services with professional discretion in relation to individual clients. On the one hand, these organizations are shaped by bureaucratic routine with an administrative structure supporting the work of the professionals. On the other, the professionals act as the link between the bureaucracy and the client. The professional task focuses on working out the best possible fit between client needs and administrative categories, an exercise Mintzberg describes as 'pigeon-holing'.

For Mintzberg the key weakness of professional bureaucracies lies in their incapacity to adapt to changing environments:

> The professional bureaucracy is an inflexible structure, well suited to producing its standard outputs but ill-suited to adopting the production of new ones. All bureaucracies are geared to stable environments; they are performance structures designed to perfect programs for contingencies that can be predicted, not problem-solving ones designed to create new programs for needs that have never before been encountered.
>
> (Mintzberg, 1983, p. 209).

The problem facing the social work professional bureaucracy in Britain in the 1970s was that it never had a chance to become accustomed to a stable environment. Scarcely had it emerged than it was confronted with new needs, new demands, challenges to professional power, changing legislative requirements and shifting budgetary constraints. Thus the social work profession was forced to try to negotiate a situation of unprecedented flux and change at a time when its bureaucratization rendered it particularly unadaptable.

Another feature of the professional bureaucracy is that it tends to develop two parallel hierarchies: one among professional staff based on expertise and experience, the other for the administrators, who provide the organizational framework within which the professionals can operate. The potential for conflict between professionals pushing for autonomy and administrators concerned with following procedures and conserving resources is evident. Yet whereas in the health service specialist doctors had combined professional prestige with administrative authority, in social work the lack of a specialist career structure meant that seniority and upward mobility tended to be reflected in a shift from the professional to the bureaucratic realm. Thus skilled and experienced social workers with leadership qualities and career ambitions tended to be rapidly promoted out of direct client work and into the administrative hierarchy. Where hospital consultants still have daily contact with patients as well as having administrative powers, social workers tended to have less and less professional contact with clients as they ascended the hierarchy.

In the new social services departments the administrators rapidly gained the upper hand over practitioners. This process was accelerated by the managerialist ethos encouraged by successive local government reorganizations and the general climate of austerity that intensified through the 1970s. One consequence of the ascendancy of the bureaucrats over the professionals was a growing polarization between social services management and the staff. This was reflected in the rapid increase in trade union membership and militancy in the new social services departments. While managers often retained their membership of the white collar local government union NALGO, the rapid influx of social workers and the much larger numbers of assistants and auxiliaries, home helps and 'meals on wheels' workers into the union led to growing internal conflicts and rising militancy. As conditions and relations deteriorated in the late 1970s a spate of often bitter and prolonged strikes ensued, further damaging the public image of social work as a profession and, in the event, generally failing to win better conditions of service or higher pay.

4   THE RADICAL CHALLENGE

Marxist politics is about the transformation of society. Marxist social work practice under capitalism aims at contributing to this transformation both by insisting on a truly human response to suffering which confronts an inhuman society and by developing, as part of the labour movement, working class struggle in the arena of welfare state apparatus.

(Corrigan and Leonard, 1978, p. 157)

Another feature of the 'professional bureaucratic' character of social work was the dependence of the profession on the state. As we have seen in Chapter 1, social work as a modern profession in Britain emerged out of the post-war children's departments and only consolidated its position through the post-Seebohm social services departments. We have also discussed the importance of social workers' statutory powers in enhancing their professional position. At the same time, social workers claimed professional expertise in dealing with areas of human experience that transcend material conditions — interpersonal relationships, experiences of loss, grief and misery, the processes of growing up and growing old. The development of a body of social work theory and casework technique enabled social workers to define clients' problems and propose solutions with considerable professional authority.

However, in the course of the 1970s, the state-based, theoretically-grounded professional status of social work came under attack from two different directions. Social work clients, both individually and collectively, began to challenge the legitimacy of social workers' definitions of their situation and needs. From within the profession itself, the radical social work movement endorsed many of these criticisms and sought to transform the theory and practice of social work.

Different client groups claimed the right to define their own needs rather than being placed in a position of dependency on social workers. People with disabilities, for example, insisted on forms of support which allowed them to take decisions, rather than being given assistance as considered appropriate by professional social workers. Many clients, from lone parents to homeless young people, in particular repudiated the tendency of social workers to reinterpret their material needs in terms of personal inadequacy. Claimants' Unions organized people dependent on welfare benefits and provided a model of self-help mobilization for other groups of recipients of various forms of social welfare services. Such challenges addressed the tension between social work's formal commitment to 'client self-determination' and its professional presumption of the wisdom and authority to understand the client's problems better than the client herself.

The influx into the rapidly expanding social services departments of a new generation radicalized by the wider trends in the student and labour movement worlds in the late sixties and early seventies created the conditions for the radical social work movement. Young social workers imbued with the optimistic spirit of the times and inspired by the promise of the Seebohm Report soon became disenchanted with the sober realities of local authority social services provision. Their alliance with radical sociologists formulated a more or less coherent critique of the emerging bureaucratic professionalism, particularly its 'hierarchical system of managerial control, coordination and supervision' (Clarke, 1979, p. 126). As Clarke noted, the increase in bureaucratic coordination and statutory requirements resulted in 'the sharpening or intensification of several professional problems and contradictions — the apparently perennial concerns about whether social work is an agency of care or control; whether its primary loyalties are to the client or to society; and over the problem of client self-determination' (ibid., p. 127).

The themes of the radical social work movement in Britain were brought together in the influential *Radical Social Work,* edited by Roy Bailey and Mike Brake in 1975, and in the follow up collection, *Radical Social Work and Practice*, published in 1980. The activist dimension of the movement was represented by the duplicated periodical *Case Con,* self-styled as 'a revolutionary magazine for social workers', which ran through twenty-five lively and provocative issues between 1970 and 1977 (Langan and Lee, 1989, p. 1).

The radical social work movement chastized post-Seebohm social work for its failure to develop a critical self-awareness and argued the need for a critical professional literature. It challenged social work's continuing preoccupation with individualistic explanations of social problems. Such notions were condemned for pathologizing the poor/deviant/victim and devaluing the role of collective political action and self-help in the attainment of humane welfare provision. The radical movement insisted that social workers needed to become less judgemental of minority lifestyles and to cultivate cultural diversity. There was also a common disaffection with the nuclear family as the basic social unit, and an aspiration to other forms of social living such as the collective or the community. The movement urged social workers to get involved in socialist political action in their own interests as well as in the interests of those who depended on their services.

The radical movement was mistrustful of the way the state used social workers to control sections of the population. It was also suspicious of professionalism among social workers, arguing that 'authentic personal relationships between client and worker' were preferable to 'relationships of professional authority' (Clark and Asquith, 1975, pp. 105–6). Radical social workers shared a 'commitment to participatory styles of decision-making within and between agencies as between social worker and client'. They often regarded their own agencies as just as big a problem as external factors.

Radical social work was always a minority movement and it lost momentum as the wider political left went into decline in the late seventies. Yet it had a lasting impact on all aspects of social work, including theory, education and the work of social services departments (Simpkin, 1989; Langan and Lee, 1989).

5 A UNITARY METHOD FOR A GENERIC PROFESSION?

Both client movements and the radical social work initiative exposed tensions and problems within state social work, focusing on the problems of professional power in particular. In this respect, they prefigured the attacks to which social work was to be subjected during the 1980s. From a variety of perspectives, social work's 'professionalism' was to be identified as a problem as we shall see in Chapters 4 and 5. But while client movements and radical social work threatened social work's fragile professional unity in the 1970s, others sought ways of strengthening it.

In parallel with the integration of personal social services and the unification of the social work profession in the wake of the Seebohm Report there was a sustained attempt to rationalize the diversity of existing social work theory and method. A core part of any professional practice is its ability to lay claim to a distinctive knowledge in advancing a field of expertise. Social work students entering the expanding range of training courses in the 1970s were confronted with the legacy of three distinct approaches — casework, groupwork and community work. Each sought to incorporate psychological and sociological theories from relevant academic disciplines to demarcate a sphere of knowledge and expertise.

Thus casework appropriated psychoanalytic theories and identified individual and family psychopathology at the root of social problems. Groupwork emerged from Klein's development of Freudian concepts in relation to group behaviour. This approach was broadened in the 1960s to include newer psychological theories — behaviour therapy, transactional analysis and learning and communication theory. Community work used sociological research to develop techniques for tackling social pathology at the local level. While the new social services departments united social work practice, proponents of the 'unitary method' attempted to rationalize social work theory (Pincus and Minahan, 1977; Goldstein, 1973; Specht, 1977; Vickery, 1977).

The 'unitary method' sought to integrate the diverse elements of social work theory in a framework provided by systems theory, itself a direct descendant of what Mishra describes as 'the dominant social theory of the two post-war decades' — functionalism (Mishra, 1983, p. 9). From this perspective, the 'system', a concept derived by analogy from a biological organism, had two distinct characteristics. First, its parts were interdependent; second, these parts tended towards preserving a state of internal equilibrium. For systems theory, as for functionalism, the commitment to order or 'maintaining equilibrium' tended to take priority over aspirations for change. For Goldstein, systems theory provided 'a framework for gaining an appreciation of the entire range of elements that bear on a social problem, including the social units involved, their expansive and dynamic characteristics, their inter-relations and the implications for change in one as it affects all others' (Goldstein, 1973, p. 110). For Pincus and Minahan 'the model' allowed for 'the selective incorporation' of particular 'theoretical orientations in working with specific situations'.

By integrating different aspects of social work knowledge the unitary approach gave the profession a more coherent foundation in theory. Goldstein acknowledged that social work was 'dependent on the social and behavioural sciences for substantive knowledge', and insisted that 'in no way does this detract from the integrity of the profession' (Goldstein, 1973, p. 68). According to Pincus and Minahan, it represented 'a reformulation of the base of social work practice' which gave social work 'a clear place among the human service professions' (Pincus and Minahan, 1977, p. 104).

The unitary approach gained popularity in the 1970s among some social workers, but particularly among social work educators who were concerned to develop an integrated social work theory as the basis for a generic professional qualification. For them the unitary approach provided a symbolic ordering of the messy reality of social work practice. It enabled them to overcome the fragmentation of social work in the 'trimethod' approach (casework, groupwork and community work) by integrating all the various ways of understanding social work into a single model. It also offered a welcome alternative to the pursuit of increasingly esoteric theories of individual and group behaviour. An important additional reason for the acceptance of the unitary approach, especially among students, was its claim to transcend the traditional focus of social work on the *individual* client. The move beyond the exclusive client focus to include a greater recognition of the community and other social and state institutions gave the unitary method a certain radical appeal. Thus even Leonard, a radical critic of the method, identified this as a potentially progressive feature (Leonard, 1975).

Others identified the fundamental defects of the unitary method in its ahistorical presumption of social harmony and eternal moral values (Langan, 1985). Following systems theory, the unitary approach assumed a biological model for the operation of society. Change is permissible within 'the system', say a family, or even an individual, but not in the structure of society as a whole, because it is assumed that the particular system must harmonize with the overall framework of society as it currently exists. The underlying assumption is that it is beneficial to restore the client's relationship with the existing society to equilibrium, whether by some minor adjustment in their outlook or circumstances. This was the crux of criticism of the unitary approach from the left and the women's movement.

Though some feminists welcomed systems theory (Osborne, 1983; Pilalis and Anderton, 1986), others considered that it endorsed the patriarchal equilibrium of modern society and was therefore disadvantageous to women's interests (Dominelli and McLeod, 1982; Langan, 1985; Marchant, 1986). According to its critics, the systems approach recommended adjustments in outlook or circumstances, which aimed to maintain or restore the status quo, thus enmeshing women more deeply in oppressive social relationships. The feminist critique of the unitary approach marked an early challenge to the project of forging a unified body of theory corresponding to the unified profession of social work. When in the 1980s other groups followed a similar course, the retreat from genericism into specialism and fragmentation gathered momentum.

6   IN CONCLUSION

> The scale of the problems, organisational constraints and inadequate training tend to throw social work into a state of confusion, helplessness and piece-meal, crisis-oriented activity similar to the state that often characterises clients, and for related reasons.
>
> (Parry, Rustin and Satyamurti, 1979, p. 63)

The social workers' strikes of the late 1970s and the election of a Conservative government on an aggressively anti-welfare programme in 1979 brought a miserable decade for social work to a grim conclusion. The establishment of a working party in October 1980 under Peter Barclay was an early response by the Government to the now universally recognized crisis of social work. In the introduction to this report, published in 1982, Barclay summed up the general perception of the problems:

> Too much is expected of social workers. We load upon them unrealistic expectations and we then complain when they do not live up to them. Social work is a relatively young profession. It has grown rapidly as the flow of legislation has greatly increased the range and complexity of its work.
>
> (Barclay, 1982, p. vii)

The introduction further discusses the 'complex pressures' facing 'large departments', identifying social workers' 'confusion about direction', their 'unease about what they should be doing and the way in which they are organised and deployed' and the difficulties of reconciling 'limitless needs' and 'inadequate resources'.

The Barclay Report attempted to reconcile Seebohm and the new right, and inevitably failed. As Smith observed, the report tried to 'preserve Seebohm's philosophy of meeting all need, whilst accepting the new right's philosophy of rolling back the state' (Smith, 1983, p. 58). Thus it made a gesture to the social democratic tradition by promoting the concept of 'community social work', which it discovered in embryo in Seebohm. It also tried to appease the Conservative government with its suggestion that if social work were directed at supporting **informal** carers, then the need for **formal** services would be reduced. The real significance of the Barclay Report, however, lies not in the main report, which by trying to please everybody suffered the fate of satisfying nobody, but in the dissenting minority reports. These were published as appendices to the main report and, not constrained by diplomatic considerations, their authors proposed bold solutions in terms which anticipated much of the subsequent debate about social work.

The first, submitted by Brown, Hadley and White, and entitled 'A case for neighbourhood-based social work and social services', broadly supported the Barclay 'community' approach but sought to take it much further, down to the neighbourhood or 'patch' level. The authors emphasized the need for radically decentralized structures to mobilize informal networks and community participation in the tasks of caring. The second, Robert Pinker's 'An alternative view', rejected both Barclay-style community social work and the patch model as likely to 'prove detrimental to the quality of social work services' (Pinker, 1982, p. 236). Pinker was particularly hostile to the patch approach:

> It conjures up the vision of a captainless crew under a patchwork ensign stitched together from remnants of the Red Flag and the Jolly Roger — all with a licence and some with a disposition to mutiny — heading in the gusty winds of populist rhetoric, with presumption as their figurehead and inexperience as their compass, straight for the reefs of public incredulity.
>
> (Pinker, 1982, p. 262)

Pinker favoured a return to traditional specialist casework, counselling the need for common sense and cautious reform.

While little is now heard of the main Barclay report, elements of both minority reports have come to enjoy greater influence in the world of social work in the past decade. What is striking is the common assumption that the experiment in providing a universal, comprehensive social work service inaugurated by Seebohm and implemented through the local authority social services departments in the 1970s is over. Both reports assume the demise of the generic social worker as the dominant force in the provision of social support. The circumstances which facilitated the further fragmentation of social work in the 1980s are the subjects of Chapters 4 and 5.

REFERENCES

Bailey, R. and Brake, M. (eds) (1975) *Radical Social Work*, London, Edward Arnold.

Barclay Report (1982) *Social Workers: their Role and Tasks*, London, National Institute for Social Work, Bedford Square Press.

Bean, P. (1979) 'The Mental Health Act 1959: rethinking an old problem', *British Journal of Law and Society*, Vol. 6.

Bean, P. (1980) *Compulsory Admissions to Mental Hospitals*, Chichester, Wiley and Sons Ltd.

Brake, M. and Bailey, R. (eds) (1980) *Radical Social Work and Practice*, London, Edward Arnold.

Brook, E. and Davis, A. (1985) 'Women and social work' in Brook, E. and Davis, A. (eds) (1985), *Women, the Family and Social Work*, London, Tavistock.

Brown, M. (1972) 'Inequality and the personal social services' in Townsend, P. and Bosanquet, N. (eds), *Labour and Inequality: Sixteen Fabian Essays*, London, Fabian Society.

Brown, P., Hadley, R., and White, K. J. (1982) 'A case for neighbourhood-based social work and social services' in Barclay Report, pp. 219–235.

Clark, C. L. and Asquith, S. (1975) *Social Work and Social Philosophy*, London, Routledge.

Clarke, J. (1979) 'Critical sociology and radical social work: problems of theory and practice' in Parry, N., Rustin, M. and Satyamurti, C. (eds), *Social Work, Welfare and the State*, London, Edward Arnold.

Clarke, J. (1980) 'Social democratic delinquents and Fabian families: a background to the 1969 Children and Young Persons Act' in *Permissiveness and Control,* London, National Deviancy Conference, Macmillan.

Clarke, J., Langan, M. and Lee, P. (1980) 'Social work: the conditions of crisis' in Carlen, P. and Collison, M. (eds) *Radical Issues in Criminology*, Oxford, Martin Robertson.

Corrigan, P. and Leonard, P. (1978) *Social Work Practice Under Capitalism: a Marxist Approach*, London, Macmillan.

Dominelli, L. and McLeod, E. (1982) 'The personal and the a-political; feminism and moving beyond the integrated methods approach' in Bailey, R. and Lee, P. *Theory and Practice in Social Work*, Oxford, Blackwell.

Donnison, D. (1968) 'Editorial', *Social Work*, October.

Goldstein, H. (1973) *Social Practice: a Unitary Approach*, Columbia, SC, University of South Carolina Press.

Hall, P. (1976) *Reforming the Welfare: The Politics of Change in the Personal Social Services*, London, Heinemann.

Ingleby Report (1960) *Report of the Committee on Children and Young Persons*, Cmnd 1191, London, HMSO.

Kilbrandon Report (1964) *Report of the Committee on Children and Young Persons (Scotland)*, Cmnd 2306, Edinburgh, HMSO.

Langan, M. (1985) 'The unitary approach: a feminist critique' in Brook, E. and Davis, A. (eds) *Women, the Family and Social Work*, London, Tavistock.

Langan, M. and Lee, P. (1989) 'Whatever happened to radical social work?' in Langan, M. and Lee, P. (eds) *Radical Social Work Today*, London, Unwin Hyman.

Leonard, P. (1975) 'Towards a paradigm for radical practice' in Bailey, R. and Brake, M., (eds) *Radical Social Work*. London, Edward Arnold.

Longford Report (1965) Home Office White Paper, Cmnd 2742, London, HMSO.

Marchant, H. (1986) 'Gender, systems thinking and radical social work' in Marchant, H. and Wearing, B. (eds) *Gender Reclaimed*, Sydney, Hale and Iremonger.

Mintzberg, H. (1983) *Structure in Fives: Designing Effective Organisations*, Englewood Cliffs, NJ, Prentice Hall.

Mishra, R. (1983) *The Welfare State in Crisis*, Brighton, Wheatsheaf Books.

NALGO (1989) *Social Work in Crisis: A Study of Conditions in Six Local Authorities*, London, NALGO.

Osborne, K. (1983) 'Women in families: feminist therapy and family systems' in *Journal of Family Therapy*, 5, pp. 1–10.

Parry, N. and Parry, P. (1979) 'Social work, professionalism and the state' in Parry, N., Rustin, M. and Satyamurti, C. (eds).

Parry, N., Rustin, M. and Satyamurti, C. (1979) 'Social work today: some problems and proposals' in Parry, N., Rustin, M. and Satyamurti, C. (eds) *Social Work, Welfare and the State*, London, Edward Arnold.

Parsloe, P. (1976) 'Social work and the justice model', *British Journal of Social Work,* Vol. 6, No. 1.

Pilalis, J. and Anderton, J. (1986) 'Feminism and family therapy — a possible meeting point', *Journal of Family Therapy*, 8, pp. 99–114.

Pincus, A. and Minahan, A. (1977) 'A model for social work practice' in Specht, H. and Vickery, A. (eds) *Integrating Social Work Methods*, London, Allen and Unwin.

Pinker, R. A. (1982) 'An alternative view' in Barclay (1982) pp. 236–62.

Seebohm Report (1968) *Report of the Committee on Local Authority and Allied Personal Social Services*, Cmnd 3703, London, HMSO.

Simpkin, M. (1989) 'Radical social work' in Carter, P., Jeffs, T., Smith, M. (eds) *Social Work and Social Welfare, Year Book 1,* Buckingham, Open University Press.

Sinfield, A. (1970) 'Which way for social work?' in Townsend, P. et al. *The Fifth Social Service: Nine Fabian Essays*, London, Fabian Society.

Smith, D. (1983) *From Seebohm to Barclay: the Changing Political Nature of the Organisation of Social Work*. Discussion paper. Department of Social Administration, University of Manchester.

Specht, H. (1977) 'Social trends' in Specht, H. and Vickery, A. (eds) *Integrating Social Work Methods*, London, Allen and Unwin.

Titmuss, R. M. (1965) 'Goals of today's welfare state' in Anderson, P. and Blackburn, R. (eds) *Towards Socialism*, London, Fontana.

Townsend, P. (1970) 'The objectives of the new local social service' in Townsend, P. et al. *The Fifth Social Service: Nine Fabian Essays,* London, Fabian Society.

Vickery, A. (1977) 'Social casework' in Specht, H. and Vickery, A. (eds).

Walton, R. (1975) *Women and Social Work*, London, Routledge & Kegan Paul.

Webb, A. (1980) 'The personal social services' in Bosanquet, N. and Townsend,P. (eds) *Labour and Equality: a Fabian Study of Labour in Power, 1974–79,* London, Heinemann.

Webb, A. and Wistow, G. (1987) *Social Work, Social Care and Social Planning: the Personal Social Services Since Seebohm*, London, Longman.

Wilding, P. (1982) *Professional Power and Social Welfare*, London, Routledge & Kegan Paul.

Younghusband Report (1959) *Report of the Working Party on Social Workers in the Local Authority Health and Welfare Services*, London, HMSO.

STUDY QUESTIONS

1   In what ways can the Kilbrandon and Seebohm Reports be said to represent the 'high tide' of professional work?

2   Why were the critics so concerned about the issue of professional power in the expansion of social work?

3   What were the main features of the criticisms of social work from client groups?

4   In what ways was the radical social work movement critical of social work?

5   What do you think were the main causes of the 'crisis of confidence' in social work?

CHAPTER 4
CHALLENGES FROM THE CENTRE

ALLAN COCHRANE

As earlier chapters have indicated, a belief in the value of professional expertise has, until recently, been one of the defining characteristics of the British welfare state — and of the social services in particular. And, as Chapter 3 argued, social workers have a special position among welfare state professionals. Their recognition as 'professionals' is a relatively recent one, a product of reorganization and expansion in the 1960s and early 1970s. This belated professionalization was also an expression of the length of time it took to move towards a more systematic organization of the personal social services and (after 1970) the creation of unified social services departments (in England and Wales) or social work departments (in Scotland) within local government, effectively taking over the social service responsibilities previously undertaken within children's, welfare, health and housing departments (and probation in Scotland). In Northern Ireland the same responsibilities are handled through appointed social services boards rather than elected local authorities.

The growth in the numbers of qualified social workers in the 1960s and 1970s was the product of state initiatives, which interacted with attempts to move towards professional status by those working as social workers. But the professional bodies of social work have never had the status of conferring licences to practise on their members. Nor have they been responsible for organizing — or accrediting — the training of social workers. That is currently the responsibility of CCETSW (Central Council for Education and Training in Social Work), which is a state appointed, but formally independent, agency, with representation from employers and educational institutions as well as professional organisations. CCETSW has defined social work as:

> ...an accountable professional activity which enables individuals, families and groups to identify personal, social and environmental difficulties adversely affecting them. Social work enables them to manage these difficulties through supportive, rehabilitative, protective or corrective action. Social work promotes social welfare and responds to wider social needs promoting equal opportunities for every age, gender, sexual preference, class, disability, race, culture and creed. Social work has the responsibility to protect the vulnerable and exercise authority under statute.   (CCETSW, 1991, p. 8)

Despite the strength of this statement, it is perhaps not surprising that social work's status remains uneasy, under question from within and without. Nor is it surprising that social work frequently seems to seek legitimation from its relationship with other (less contested) professions from time to time, including psychology (see Chapter 2), medicine and the law. It is, however, one of the minor ironies of history that, just as social work managed to drag itself into the apparently calm waters of public sector professionalism at the start of the 1970s, all the certainties of the welfare state on which such professionalism was based themselves began to be undermined.

The problems of the British welfare state since the mid-1970s have been well documented (see for example, **Clarke and Langan, 1993a and b**). A combination of financial pressures, political criticism and professional self-doubt helped to raise questions about the old arrangements, although often without clarifying what better ones would look like. In this chapter and the next we shall set out to explore some of the pressures which were faced by social work through the 1980s and into the 1990s. This has been and continues to be a period of substantial upheaval for social services departments and other providers of social services. Past practices have been scrutinized and questioned. Social work and social workers have frequently found themselves on the front pages of newspapers and the subject of various forms of judicial inquiry. They have had to live with the consequences and uncertainties of organizational change, whether encouraged by the introduction of new official guidelines, or imposed through legislation, such as the National Health Service and Community Care Act 1990 and the Children Act 1989 (in England and Wales. At the time of writing similar legislation is promised for Scotland on the basis of a White Paper published in 1992). Attempts have increasingly been made to transform the ways in which social services are organized, managed and delivered.

In this chapter attention will be focused on the challenges to social work which have come from above: that is from central government and political parties, but also arising out of a range of other state and judicial interventions. The focus will, therefore, be on politicians and others within the policy community. We will be seeking to identify the sources of these challenges and shall allow those making them to speak in their own words, represented by official documents and statements. One of the issues which will run through the chapter is the extent to which challenges from the centre have helped to reshape the nature of contemporary social work. In the next chapter (Chapter 5) George Taylor will consider the ways in which social work has responded to rather different sets of challenges — from the margins, from the 'users' rather than the providers or managers of social work.

The next section of this chapter looks directly at the changing political context for social work, largely as expressed in the arguments of the Conservative governments of the 1980s. It therefore draws on the open statements of party politics. The following section (Section 2) takes rather a different approach, looking at the ways in which a wider (and less controversial in party political terms) set of moves towards 'community care' developed, apparently bringing state and profession closer together. Section 3 shifts once more to look at the influence of judicial and quasi-judicial inquiries and the rise of inter-agency working, in the particular context of child protection work. Finally, Section 4 points forward to considerations about the future of social work which are taken up again in Chapter 6.

I   THE CRISES OF WELFARISM: POLITICAL ATTACKS

It is important to set out the challenges to welfare professionals, and to social workers in particular, in the context of the wider initiatives associated with the Thatcher governments of the 1980s, even if some of the political questioning had begun well before the election of Margaret Thatcher as Prime Minister in 1979. It is probably unhelpful and certainly unnecessary to look for some wholly consistent programme of 'Thatcherism' or of the 'new right' which was being implemented through the 1980s. Not only is the logic of policy formation and implementation rarely as clear cut as such formulations imply, but it is also generally a fruitless task to search for the underlying truth (or underlying logic) encapsulated in political philosophies such as these. One consequence of such a focus is that it becomes rather too tempting to look for and find the (inevitable) gap between the reality of implementation and the idealized programme of government or political party, which has itself usually been defined by academics and political analysts rather than the protagonists themselves. Nevertheless it is possible, more modestly, to identify some general features in the political rhetoric of the period and the changing welfare policies associated with it. Setting the context in this way should make it easier to understand the environment to which social workers and social work managers were forced to adapt if they wanted to survive.

Four features of the politics which dominated in the 1980s are particularly significant here and are spelled out below. First — and this was an argument which was already important in the second half of the 1970s — it was maintained that it was increasingly difficult to pay the costs of maintaining the welfare state. In its strongest version, this argument was taken further to suggest that one of the reasons for the weakness of the UK economy was that a bloated (and unproductive) public sector was undermining the profitability of the private sector on which a healthy economy was said to rely. This was summed up in the title of one book which received a great deal of attention in the late 1970s: *Britain's Economic Problem: Too Few Producers* (Bacon and Eltis, 1976). But even where this conclusion was not drawn (that is, even if the cause of economic crisis was explained differently), there was increasing agreement across political parties (admittedly, expressed most forcefully from within the Conservative Party) that levels of state spending had to be reduced. This was taken to imply that welfare state spending had to be reduced. One of the first objects of attack from the centre was local government spending, which it was argued (by Labour as well as Conservative ministers) had risen far more than was justified. Since spending on social services was the second largest category of local authority expenditure (after education) this meant that it was subject to financial restraint throughout the period from 1976 onwards. In other words, almost as soon as the role of social work was given formal institutional recognition in the wake of the Seebohm and Kilbrandon Reports, financial considerations began to place significant constraints on the ways in which social workers were able to develop their practice.

The second important argument within Conservative politics in the 1980s was that the welfare state effectively operated as what was often called a 'nanny' state. Because it provided financial and other support, it was argued that the state undermined the will of welfare recipients to seek work and — more important — to take responsibility for their own lives (the welfare state was frequently blamed for creating an 'underclass' of welfare dependants, see **Cochrane, 1993**). 'Helping people,' it was suggested, 'weakens the will to self-help' (Seldon, 1982, p. 8). Rhodes Boyson, a Conservative MP who was later a Minister for Social Security for a short time in the 1980s, expressed this view particularly strongly at an early stage:

> The moral fibre of our people has been weakened. The State which does for its citizens what they can do for themselves is an evil state; and a state which removes all choice and responsibility from its people and makes them like broiler hens will create the irresponsible society. No-one cares, no-one saves, no-one bothers — why should they when the state spends all its energies taking money from the energetic, successful and thrifty to give to the idle, the failures and the feckless?
>
> (Boyson, 1971, p. 5).

Margaret Thatcher made similar criticisms in a speech to the Greater London Young Conservatives in July 1976 which set out her vision of welfare and emphasized the importance of personal rather than state responsibility:

> Choice in a free society implies responsibility. There is not a hard and fast line between economic and other forms of personal responsibility to self, family, firm, community, nation, God. Morality lies in choosing between feasible alternatives. A moral being is one who exercises his own judgement in choices on matters great and small, bearing in mind their moral dimension, i.e. right and wrong. In so far as his right and duty is taken away by the State, the party or the union, his moral faculties — his capacity for choice — atrophy and he becomes a moral cripple.
>
> (quoted in Russell, 1978, p. 104).

Mixed in with this generalized criticism of the welfare state, there were also implications about the role of social workers: at best they were misguided do-gooders, mistakenly believing that they were helping people when they were not; at worst they were interfering in ways which were resented by those they claimed to be helping and were, in practice, probably making matters worse for them. As we shall see, this was also a theme which emerged in some of the public inquiries into child abuse cases in the 1980s.

Although not explicitly stated in official arguments, it is difficult to avoid the conclusion that one aspect of the criticism was related to the overwhelming feminization of social work — at the level of fieldworker if not at more senior levels. The implication was that social work was an illegitimate profession, precisely because it was largely made up of women — and relatively young and 'inexperienced' women at that — who could not be expected to understand the complexities (and responsibilities) of family life.

This set of concerns led into a third theme, namely the desire to move welfare out of the hands of state institutions whether by mobilizing 'care in the community' or by encouraging the growth of voluntary provision. Like the concern about spending levels, this was a theme which was taken up across the political spectrum, although there were significant differences in emphasis between political parties. The notion of an 'enabling authority' was developed to encapsulate this shift in local government and Margaret Thatcher herself endorsed it early in the decade, commenting that: 'I am very encouraged by the way in which local authorities, Directors of Social Services, the social work profession and the specialist press are increasingly determined to shift the emphasis of statutory provision so that it becomes an enabling service, a statutory provision enabling the volunteers to do their job more effectively' (quoted in Loney, 1986, p. 134).

The political pressures were clear enough, encouraging a move away from direct state provision, towards the development of 'enabling' authorities whose role was to encourage welfare recipients to move away from dependency to forms of self-help as well as to 'enable' other (non-state) organizations to deliver social services. Those would include private sector contractors and voluntary organizations, the larger of which might more accurately (to use a term first developed in the US) be described as 'not-for-profit organizations', since most of those working for them were paid employees rather than volunteers. These political initiatives were not explicitly targeted against social workers: in principle it is not too difficult to imagine them having responsibilities stretching across the state, private and voluntary sectors. But since the initiatives were developed in the context of a wider Government hostility to 'state bureaucracies' it is difficult not to conclude that one (welcome) consequence was likely to be a weakened social work profession. Certainly as expressed by those speaking on behalf of the Conservative governments of the 1980s and early 1990s there can be little doubt that the reforms were seen as part of a process of undermining what were seen as the monolithic professions of the welfare state, particularly the local welfare state.

This is brought out clearly in a report by N. Wood published in *The Times* in 1991:

■ MUNICIPAL armies of social workers should be disbanded and responsibility for caring for the vulnerable and inadequate transferred to smaller community-based groups, a senior minister said yesterday.

John Patten questioned whether so much social care should still be in the hands of the state. Big municipal social services departments, with up to 10,000 staff, were no longer the right agencies to tackle problems such as child abuse, poverty and homelessness. Their duties should be handed over to 'care associations' modelled on housing associations, to make services more responsive to their clients and needs.

Mr Patten, a prime candidate for promotion to the cabinet in the next reshuffle, from his post as a Home Office minister of state, argued that such an upheaval would be in tune with the radical changes made by the Conservatives in the 1980s. Power was being taken away from state bureaucracies in areas such as health and education and handed to consumers. The same thinking should now be applied to other public services.

Mr Patten predicted that this notion of 'participation', the unsung big idea of the late 1980s, would take off in the decade ahead. It could do for social policy what privatization had done for the economy.

'This is a new agenda which requires rather more opportunity and effort than money; is in tune with the times; has started to happen here and there; and is eminently achievable in a decade,' he said in the latest edition of *Newsline*, the Tory party newspaper. 'It is a matter not just of asking active citizens to lend more of their time to those who need it, but the beginnings of a positive process which could be a powerful partner to privatisation — giving back power to people over their own communities, and a new edge to Conservative thinking.'

'Is it really necessary for some of our big cities to have approaching 10,000 or so social workers and related staff on their payrolls?'

'Are such large groups of people appropriate, any more than it is appropriate for one local authority to own vast holdings of council houses and flats?'

'The housing association idea could be used to dissect these big empires, giving much more small-scale, local involvement over how such help is provided. Perhaps the next decade will see the burgeoning of care associations, breaking down local authority monopolies, bringing the help closer to local people; a help which is as intimate in style as possible.'

(The Times, 3 January 1991.) ■

(At the time — as the report indicates — John Patten was a Minister of State at the Home Office. In 1992 he became Secretary of State at the Department of Education.)

Although the proposals discussed in the above newspaper report are not exclusively directed at social work, it is not too difficult to see what some of the results of their implementation might be. Since the development of social work has been tied up very closely with the development and expansion of social services departments in the context of the welfare state, so the fragmentation and break up of those departments is also likely to make it more difficult to sustain or identify a reasonably consistent professional core.

This leads into the fourth aspect of the political arguments which developed through the 1980s. As well as challenging the organization and delivery of social work as a state provided 'service', they also began to question the value of the 'profession' itself, for example by suggesting that some of the things traditionally done by social services departments (and, by implication, by professional social workers) could instead be done by others.

Professionals were held to have interests of their own in expanding state provision to increase their status and improve their career prospects. In one publication of the Social Affairs Unit (an influential 'new right' lobby group on welfare issues), Lait argued that the move towards generic social work at the end of the 1960s was simply part of a process of professional aggrandizement. It took place, she suggested, in response to growing popular criticisms of existing child care services which were proving unable to meet the expectations which they had themselves raised. Instead of concluding that professional intervention through individual casework was inappropriate and unhelpful (Lait's own view), professionals were able to turn matters around to argue that everything would be better if professionally trained social workers were able to operate across a wider field in a unified department, working with families, providing welfare support, dealing with issues of mental health, and the problems of older people, coordinating provision and assessing need.

According to the dominant professional arguments, said Lait, the reason for past lack of success was that child care social workers had been restricted to far too narrow an area of responsibility and that other areas had been left to workers who did not have adequate professional training. Instead of moving away from social work intervention into families through casework (that is recognizing their failure), Lait suggested that child care professionals and their trainers sought to bolster their position by calling for the spread of their forms of training across the social work spectrum. She neatly summarizes her argument as follows:

> Predictably enough, since unattainable objectives proved absolutely unattainable, workers and trainers united in their discontent to demand first that departments should be unconditionally released from the straitjacket of Child Care, and second that training of a 'generic' nature should replace the old specialisms. After much lobbying, and gross over-representation of the profession on the Seebohm Committee, their wish was granted.
>
> (Lait, 1981, p. 36).

It was suggested that many aspects of the social work role were not really 'professional' at all, but rather at best an expression of common sense (and at worst merely self-serving). As a result, such tasks might be handled better by people with no professional aspirations, whether through informal care (for example, within the family) or by part-time and voluntary 'carers' who, it was argued, might even be more in touch with the practical needs of those being served. Towards the end of a sustained polemic criticizing the practice and theory of social work (for being confused and claiming to be able to deliver far more than it can), Brewer and Lait comment that for old people 'visits from social workers may be better than no visits at all, but the evidence is that the services needed are practical and can be provided by competent untrained officials, who are just as likely to be kindly, sympathetic people as are social workers, and marginally more likely to be reliable' (Brewer and Lait, 1980, p. 210).

In this perspective, the value of a person-based 'expertise' like that identified by Roger Sapsford in Chapter 2 is significantly reduced. Within the 'enabling' authority, the role of social services departments is seen to be one of managing rather than providing welfare or — to use the language which has increasingly been adopted — care services. Legislation and government guidelines on community care now talk of care managers, rather than social workers. The key skills are increasingly identified as those of managing a range of different providers (preparing plans for individual cases) and of effectively contributing to a wider network of inter-agency working (see Sections 3 and 4 below) rather than those of case work or any form of therapeutic intervention. If therapy is needed the expectation is that it will be 'bought in' from another agency.

The pressures we have identified so far have come from the political level: in particular from the Conservative governments of the 1980s. It is, however, important to acknowledge that they did not just come from the Conservative Party or the 'new right' but had a wider resonance within policy communities and in other political parties. The changes cannot simply be explained as an expression of the policies of the 'new right' — or at any rate, the policies of the 'new right' themselves may need to be understood as just one expression of wider shifts within the welfare state. The challenge to social work as a profession was both an expression of and a part of the restructuring of the British welfare state which began in the mid-1970s. This is apparent not only in the language and debates of the politicians but also in some of the ways in which critiques developed from within the welfare state itself, in particular within professional and official debates. And it is to these that we turn next.

2   MOVING TOWARDS 'CARE IN THE COMMUNITY'

The notion of community care became the dominant organizing principle — perhaps better described as a slogan — around which the reshaping of local welfare services took place through the 1980s and into the 1990s. It was increasingly taken for granted that care in the community was better for those requiring long term welfare support than the provision of residential care by the state in institutions or 'homes'. One of the main professional journals targeted at social workers is even called *Community Care*. Moving towards community care has been a stated ambition of government, health authorities and local councils since the 1960s, but it was only when it was linked to ways of reducing levels of public spending that the process of change began to accelerate. In the late 1980s the Griffiths Report on care in the community commented that: 'community care has been talked about for thirty years and in few areas can the gap between political rhetoric and policy on the one hand, or between policy and reality in the field on the other hand have been so great'. The report went on to identify 'a feeling that community care is a poor relation; everybody's poor relative but nobody's baby' (Griffiths, 1988, para. 9). It was not until the Conservative governments of the 1980s that it seems to have become an idea whose time had come, in large part because it was possible for members of those governments (such as John Patten, quoted above) to reinterpret community care as another means of moving away from direct state provision towards the more explicit recognition of a mixed economy of welfare, in which the state's role would become less significant (see also Audit Commission, 1986).

But it was also a view which gained increasing support within the institutions and professions of the welfare state at the same time. Across a range of disciplines it came to be accepted that individuals and groups defined as problems (or facing problems) could best be 'treated' in a community context. This became the orthodoxy not only for work with older people, mentally ill people (see **Dallos and Boswell, 1993**), people with physical or learning disabilities, but also in working with juvenile offenders (see **McLaughlin and Muncie, 1993**) and in child care work. Care in the community was broadly defined as almost anything which did not involve the provision of state run institutional care (including prisons and other forms of youth custody). In other words, it stretched from an increased reluctance to take children into residential care, to encouraging older people and people with disabilities to remain in their homes, to support for the conversion of Victorian houses into hostels for people with learning difficulties and young people being moved out of residential care. In principle, there was recognition of the need to recognize the role of informal carers (such as children, partners, and friends), of the need to provide flexible support (for example, through home helps) and even of the extent to which these tasks usually seemed to be the responsibility of women. In practice there were continuing doubts about whether formal recognition would be translated into an adequate allocation of resources to support informal care.

Some aspects of this new orthodoxy might be expected to fit in well with the notion of social work as a profession since it starts from assumptions about the need for individualized intervention targeted on people in their own homes rather than in residential care. And, in principle, it has certainly been welcomed by professional organizations. Under the National Health Service and Community Care Act 1990, the role of lead agency in the field of community care is taken by local social services authorities.

There has also been some transfer of resources from health authorities and boards to local authorities (or social services boards in Northern Ireland). The payment for private or voluntary sector residential accommodation for old people is handled through these agencies too. In other words, social services departments are given a central role within the new arrangements (see also Griffiths, 1988; HMSO, 1989). Since most social workers currently work in social services (in England and Wales) or social work departments (in Scotland), therefore, one might expect moves such as these to increase their status.

But in practice matters have not been so simple, in large part because community care also implies a move away from traditional forms of specialist professional expertise. This was already clear in a statement of the objectives of community care made by the Department of Health and Social Security in the early 1980s.

■ [These objectives were:]

- to enable an individual to remain in his own home wherever possible, rather than being cared for in a hospital or residential home;

- to give support and relief to informal carers (family, friends and neighbours) coping with the stress of caring for a dependent person;

- to deliver appropriate help, by the means which cause the least possible disruption to ordinary living;

- to relieve the stresses and strains contributing to or arising from physical or emotional disorder;

- to provide the most cost-effective package of services to meet the needs and wishes of those being helped;

- to integrate all the resources of a geographical area in order to support the individuals within it. The resources might include informal carers, NHS and personal social services and organized voluntary effort, but also sheltered housing, the local social security office, the church, local clubs, and so on.

(Evidence to the House of Commons Committee on Social Services, HC13 1984–85. Quoted in Griffiths, 1988, pp. 5-6). ■

The Griffiths Report on community care went further than this to argue for a comprehensive system, much of which found legislative expression in the National Health Service and Community Care Act 1990 (implemented in 1993). Above all the report argued for a move away from the existing arrangements in which services (outside Northern Ireland) were largely provided directly by local authority social services or social work departments to one in which the departments took on a more strategic role, identifying needs and purchasing services from a range of other agencies, groups and even individuals:

■   Local social services authorities should, within the resources available:

1   assess the community care needs of their locality, set local priorities and service objectives, and develop local plans in consultation with health authorities in particular (but also others including housing authorities, voluntary bodies, and private providers of care) for delivering those objectives;

2   identify and assess individuals' needs, taking full account of personal preferences (and those of informal carers), and design packages of care best suited to enabling the consumer to live as normal a life as possible;

3   arrange the delivery of packages of care to individuals, building first on the available contribution of informal carers and neighbourhood support, then the provision of domiciliary and day services or, if appropriate, residential care;

4   act for these purposes as the designers, organizers and purchasers of non-health care services, and not primarily as direct providers, making the maximum possible use of voluntary and private sector bodies to widen consumer choice, stimulate innovation and encourage efficiency.

(Griffiths, 1988, p. 1).   ■

The Act requires social services departments to prepare community care plans which project future needs and indicate how they might be met, in particular showing how departments will call on private and voluntary agencies to deliver services. The Griffiths Report acknowledges that the new arrangements are likely to change the ways in which professionals — and social workers in particular — will have to operate.

■   The proposals involve significant changes in role for a number of professional and occupational groups. In many cases their implementation will more sharply focus developments which are already taking place within professions. For example, many social services staff already have a managerial function, but my approach will give this added emphasis, for example in the development of the skills needed to buy in services. Other new skills, particularly in the design of successful management accounting systems and the effective use of the information produced by them, will be needed. The change in role of social services authorities might also allow them to make more productive use of the management abilities and experience of all their staff, including those who are not qualified social workers.
(Griffiths, 1988, p. 25).   ■

Without always being stated explicitly, community care, as expressed in the Griffiths Report and the NHS and Community Care Act, implies a clear and unequivocal move away from approaches to social work which are based on medical and psychiatric or therapeutic models and stress the importance of case work. Instead social workers — possibly renamed care managers — are intended to act as coordinators putting together packages of care for individuals on the basis of assessments of need and identifying others (whether within their department or outside it) to meet those needs. In this model, a clear distinction is made between 'purchaser' and 'provider'.

In principle, care managers are expected to become the purchasers of services provided by others, whether employed by the direct services parts of social services departments, by various forms of trust (including hospital trusts) and voluntary agencies, or by private sector organizations (for example, in the form of residential care). In Northern Ireland (despite some legal difficulties) moves were already taking place in the early 1990s to set up social services trusts along similar lines to those already operating in the health service. These will in a sense be contracted by social service boards to operate the social services system (covering community care and child protection), but will themselves act as purchasers in ensuring the delivery of particular services.

The split between 'purchaser' and 'provider' also effectively splits the traditional social work role, emphasizing the extent of the change within the UK's existing 'mixed economy of welfare'. Although — of course — social workers have always drawn on contributions from other agencies in dealing with many of their cases, they remained responsible for them and generally saw themselves (and were seen) as contributing more than assessment in working with families and 'clients'.

If social workers are redefined as care managers — as 'purchasers' — then the balance of their professional role seems to shift explicitly to one of management, even if it is 'management' of a rather particular type. Not surprisingly, therefore, the Griffiths Report argues for courses in management to be added to qualifying and in-service training for social workers (although this recommendation does not seem to be reflected in the requirements laid down by CCETSW for the Diploma in Social Work (CCETSW, 1991).

In such a model, care managers are expected to have the key skills of being able to assess what services are required in individual cases; to make judgements about how (and by whom) those services may be delivered; to manage budgets in ways which ensure that appropriate services can be provided without disadvantaging others; and to monitor the ways in which services are provided. Meanwhile the management of care managers is seen to have less and less to do with any residual social work professional expertise and might even be taken on by managers who do not have any direct experience of social work. Even if such experience continues to be expected by appointments committees, the gap between the practice of strategic management and that of field social work — particularly as undertaken by 'providers' and 'carers' — is likely to be very wide. One Audit Commission report argues that care managers should not be social workers and that 'social work...is a provision in its own right, to be commissioned by the care manager, although the role of care manager may well encompass a degree of counselling and support' (Audit Commission, 1992, p. 27).

The status of 'provider' in the community care model is an uneasy and uncertain one. It is generally defined — implicitly at least — in ways which suggest that the skills associated with 'caring' are not really 'professional' at all. One result of finally acknowledging the vital part which has always been played by informal care (that is usually provided by women to other members of their families) in the mixed economy of welfare has been to undermine the position of 'professionals' (who, in this case, are also generally women). Fragmenting the various aspects of provision so that they only come together in packages of care managed from above suggests that each can be handled individually by different and, by definition, 'unskilled' providers or carers operating on the basis of common sense and not professional training. Paradoxically, too, however, such an arrangement is unlikely to 'empower' carers or service users since the level and form of resources allocated to them will depend not on their own demands or self-activity, but on the decisions of those making assessments and managing scarce resources.

Only where the role of providers can be defined as reflecting special expertise will they be able to create a stronger professional identity for themselves. The importance of medical expertise, for example, is likely to be given still more status, and the implications of the Children Act 1989 are that social workers working with child abuse may need to have had extensive specialist training in addition to their basic generic qualification. The argument for such training is developed in a collection of papers published by CCETSW (Peitroni, 1991; see also Department of Health, 1988) and arguments for specialist social workers are also considered in a report prepared by Directors of Social Work in Scotland, although new legislation had not yet been introduced there when the report was written (Directors of Social Work in Scotland, 1992, pp. 22–3). Those supporting increased specialization suggest — among other arguments — that it 'leads to increased knowledge, expertise and professional satisfaction' (Directors of Social Work in Scotland, 1992, p. 22).

The other side of the rearrangements is a renewed emphasis on inter-agency collaboration and joint working, although references to the need for joint planning date back to the 1970s. In community care this has been particularly focused on collaboration between local authorities, family health service authorities, health authorities and health boards. Although the legislation and the Griffiths Report both suggest that local authorities — social services or social work departments — should be lead agencies in the development of community care, in practice the legislation also encourages health authorities to define their roles more widely, because they are no longer simply concerned with the provision of clear cut medical or health services, but are encouraged to take a more holistic view, seeking to improve primary health care, thus reducing the need for direct medical intervention. There has been a significant growth of joint planning teams covering policy areas such as people with physical or learning disabilities, mental health and the care of old people. In many areas, health authorities have begun to develop local planning initiatives in which they play the lead role, organizing activity around issues of primary health care and drawing in other agencies (including social services departments) as part of this. The implication of such moves is that medical rather than social work concerns (and professionals) may be expected to dominate. One District Health Manager went so far as to raise another possible consequence, suggesting that 'It would be nice if we could keep local politics out of this altogether' (Nichols, 1991, p. 5).

Even if social services departments are to be successful in retaining the lead role, they clearly have to negotiate with other agencies, including voluntary bodies and the private sector as well as health authorities, in preparing community care plans as well as in the practice of welfare provision. The moves towards inter-agency working, like other aspects of the community care reforms, also represent challenges to traditional interpretations of the social work role. The specific skills of social work do not seem to be valued significantly in such a model. On the contrary, not only does it imply that a range of agencies are required to deal with particular problems, but the skills which appear to become most highly valued are those of managing budgets, managing collaboration and understanding management information systems. The skills whose value is being questioned are those of case work, which have traditionally been associated with social work, and the growth of inter-agency working may even call the assessment role into question, as it has to be shared with other sets of professionals (and other carers). Some of the consequences of moving towards increased inter-agency working can be seen more clearly and are developed more fully in the next section, which focuses on the child protection system and its operation.

3   CHILD PROTECTION: RESPONDING TO INQUIRIES

3.1   THE IMPACT OF THE INQUIRIES

The 1980s were a decade of inquiries into and reports on many aspects of social work practice which helped to create a beleaguered context for the profession throughout the UK. The decade began with an attempt by the social work profession to identify a new role for itself (Barclay, 1982) and ended with that role being more clearly specified in government statutes and circulars on the basis of reports such as Griffiths (1988) and Audit Commission (1986). At any one time social workers always seemed to be waiting for another inquiry report to be published just as the previous one was being digested. Social work was a profession whose members were continually being forced to reassess their practice. There were major inquiries into residential social work, where scandals uncovered included those which identified systematic physical and sexual abuse of children as well as the more mundane realities of disciplinary regimes which abused children in less obvious ways. But probably the most widely reported inquiries were those which focused on child abuse within families and the failure of state agencies to deal with it appropriately (see also **Saraga, 1993**). In the 1970s and early 1980s most of them were concerned with child deaths (and tended to criticize social workers for failure to intervene), whilst those of the late 1980s were more likely to be focused on cases of alleged sexual abuse (and tended to criticize social workers for intervening too readily and with insufficient evidence). It is perhaps also worth noting that many of the earlier inquiries were concerned with cases of children in lone-parent families or in which the parents were unmarried. Many of the children involved were Afro-Caribbean (or described as 'mixed race'). The later inquiries dealt with children in families which looked more like the traditional 'nuclear' model, and most of the children were white. These differences may also help to explain some of the differences in the attitude to intervention expressed in the inquiries. The best known of the inquiries of the late 1980s was the judicial inquiry into events in Cleveland in 1987 where there was 'an unprecedented rise in the diagnosis of child sexual abuse during the months of May and June' (Butler-Sloss, 1988, p.1).

The form generally taken by the inquiries was one which itself implied a direct challenge to social work, because it was based on the norms and practices of the legal system (with its stress on rules and rights rather than evaluating balances of probability about what might be in a child's best interests). Some (like the Cleveland inquiry and more recently the inquiry chaired by Lord Clyde into the handling of allegations of ritual abuse in the Orkneys) have been explicitly judicial and others (like that into the death of Jasmine Beckford chaired by Louis Blom-Cooper), although sponsored by local authorities, have borrowed the judicial model. The use of the Social Services Inspectorate to investigate social work practice in Rochdale at the end of the 1980s represents an alternative approach, but it also points towards the possibility of a more consistent form of monitoring and investigation from above, possibly implying a more limited degree of autonomy for professionals at the bottom (Social Services Inspectorate, 1990).

The eighteen inquiry reports into child abuse which were published in the 1980s have been comprehensively summarized in a report published by the Department of Health (1991). This report highlights some of the limitations associated with the various inquiries, noting the feeling of inadequacy left by the gap between the harrowing accounts of particular cases and the policy proposals which stem from them. Each inquiry report was specific, and it sometimes seems not only that their cumulative recommendations were inconsistent, but also that — despite the high profiles many of them had — they were only relevant to a very limited area of social work. The Department of Health summary report also expresses concern about the extent to which inquiries help to make people feel as if 'something is being done' while also emphasizing the role of social workers (and other professionals) as social police:

■ The impact of reading the inquiries *en bloc* and by chronological date of publication is very considerable.

The stories of the individual children are moving and the tragedy of the death, usually described near the middle of the report, ...always [has a] moving impact. Afterwards, reading the policy and practice discussion seems rather superfluous. What really can be done? In the end, after the policy points have been taken on board or left as too case-specific, the stories of the children remain. Too few case studies of abused children are in the public domain and the inquiries are worth reading in full for them.

THE LIMITS OF THE INQUIRIES:

The task of this report — identifying key lessons to be learned — rather assumes that they have not been learned. There is no way of knowing. There is no mechanism by which practice is monitored nationally or even a medium within which good case practice is routinely encouraged to be brought forward and published.

The inquiries vary in length from 20 to 300 pages and make from 4 to 90 recommendations. They take differing views about the breadth of their remit, and clearly find it difficult to generalize from an individual case about how services and organizations should operate. Generalising from 'failure' is self-evidently unsound. Moreover, the information available to the inquiry is partial. In a number of inquiries key players in the inter-agency network were not prepared to give evidence.

Other limitations are more profound. The inquiries focus on child abuse as a product of family interaction, and focus on members of the family as recipients of services following a point of referral. The effects of this are to exclude an analysis of child abuse within social structure, class, race and gender. The effects of environmental disadvantage are not generally analysed, and when referred to are with difficulty, if at all, tied into what happened. Secondly, analysing families as recipients of services excludes what services might have helped prevent the abuse if they had been made available. Thirdly, an analysis of what happened to the family as *people* rather than recipients of services is not found. The quest for understanding about why children are killed by some people and not others is scarcely taken forward. What models of child abuse can integrate social deprivation and individual pathology? How do we understand the family as a forum for child abuse? How do we interpret what we hear particularly from children?

A further limitation is to be found in the form which inquiries take — geared up to an adversarial process overseen by lawyers. The inquiries reflect upon themselves at considerable length — discussing the benefits of being held in private or public, the most effective manner of taking evidence, and the nature of their accountability. A theme running through this analysis of themselves...[is] concern about delays in starting, concern about information being made available to it, and concern about how to obtain the attendance of key people. The resulting [report] is something of a view of what happened, and who was to blame — rather than why.

It might reasonably be argued, in defence of inquiries, that they cannot be expected to analyse everything about child abuse — they cannot adopt that breadth of remit, and they are not primarily training or research, or even practice development aids. They are about the delivery of local services to a family in which a child abuse death occurred. In these terms, a key issue needs to be addressed further. That is the relationship between policies, procedures and practices of individual agencies in relation to child protection how these relate to the law, in particular to the statutory duties of the local authority and the most effective way in which the agencies can work together.

THE INQUIRIES IN CONTEXT

It does seem as though the child abuse inquiries have a life and history of their own. Writers in the field of social policy have variously identified the unintended and negative consequences of the child abuse inquiry, in particular the way in which they define child abuse in terms of individual pathology, how they...[tend] to emphasize the role of caring professions as 'social policing', and how they serve to give the community a feeling of doing something in a climatic or moral panic. Two points have struck most forcibly.

First, the fragmentation — isolation — of child protection services from the rest of child care. The inquiries are only the most extreme form of special arrangements — legal and administrative, for scrutinizing for child protection services as distinct from the rest of the services which children in need should receive. This is not just an academic or ideological point. Its practical application, for example in the way professions advise and assist the local authority, and meet together in a case conference or case review context — directly affects services received by the child and family.

Secondly, the inquiries represent in an extreme form the polarization of points of view, and of people, in a framework that is supposed to bring people into working together. This is not just reflected in the adversarial nature of the inquiries but also in the stance of the media to these major public events, and in the polarization of the children's interests versus the parents' interests versus public interests versus professional interests.

(Department of Health, 1991, pp. 109–10.) ■

One of the problems with the reports which were produced is that each focused on only one incident, which meant that they managed to produce a generalized feeling of uncertainty about how social workers should behave as well as a feeling that the profession was under siege, without at the same time succeeding in producing any clear general guidelines about how to improve matters. In many of the inquiries into the deaths of children (such as those on Jasmine Beckford, Kimberley Carlile, Lucy Gates and Heidi Koseda, as well as the earlier report on the case of Maria Colwell) stress was placed on the need for social workers to intervene more actively and to challenge the statements of parents more forcibly. Concern was expressed that the therapeutic assumptions of social work practice tended to encourage social workers to seek to maintain friendly relations with parents at the expense of the interests of their children. In the Cleveland report — on the contrary — it was argued that too little attention had been paid to the need to maintain positive relationships with parents. Similar points were made in reports which followed Cleveland, referred back to it and were also largely concerned with child sexual abuse, rather than physical abuse or the deaths of children.

Despite the differences between them, however, one of the results of the cluster of inquiries has been to reinforce moves towards the development of more detailed codes of practice and increasingly prescriptive guidelines (which may themselves then be taken into account in legal cases, for example, when parents challenge social services or social work departments). In other words the scope for autonomous (professional) decision making at local level has been reduced, and — in principle at least — it is easier for social workers to be challenged if they do not follow the rules.

Again this shift is explicitly noted in the points made by the Department of Health report:

■ The most important single outcome from the inquiries of the 80s has been the establishment of a set of principles for professional relationships to parents and children, in the Cleveland report. Yet if this is to be more than a convention of good manners strategies for turning policy to practice and sharing best practice, nationally, need to be developed. Lessons are to be learned elsewhere than the child abuse inquiries: the funding of research; the promulgation of information — both about individual inquiries and developing practice; and most importantly the way in which organizations 'learn' about themselves and monitor performance and improve standards of practice.

There is a view that child care and child protection are solely — at best mainly — the prerogative of the welfare agencies. Of course this is not so. It is parents who kill their children, not professional agencies. Yet it is a reflection on the fragmentation of the care of children within our society that welfare agencies are howlingly blamed when 'things go wrong'. The public is ambivalent about what it wants from services — in particular how intrusive into families professional workers should be, and how much services should cost. At the same time we are ambivalent about child abuse. 'The child is a person and not an object of concern' has become the motto for child protection services in the late 80s. How this is put into effect by professionals, the public, parents and children to inform the delivery of services case by case, is the key question for preventing child abuse and protecting children in the 90s.

(Department of Health, 1991, pp. 111–12) ■

Another issue on which there seems to have been agreement was that social workers faced major problems in handling the multiple roles with which they were charged. Indeed, the implication seems to be that they were often set impossible tasks. This comes out very clearly in summaries of the different reports:

■   Double standards operate in the field of child protection. Many of the inquiries note the difficulties in, and complexities of, social work tasks. The final submission to the Cleveland inquiry of the Social Services Department pointed out 'the Social Services, of course, always have a thankless task. If they are over-cautious and take children away from their families they are pilloried for doing so. If they do not take such action and do not take the child away from the family and something terrible happens to the child, then likewise they are pilloried' (Butler-Sloss, 1988, p.88). At the same time inquiries recognize there is no way in which social services departments can effectively monitor a situation so as to prevent the child dying in consequences or incidents of violence and injuries, except by removing that child from home altogether (Liam Johnson, 1989, 3.94).

The Kimberley Carlile inquiry considered that social workers are entitled to some special treatment when it comes to public accountability. 'As a class of public servants they are patronised by professionals in the law and in medicine; they are vilified by the popular press; they are disliked by sections of the public who misunderstand, or are ignorant of what social work is about; their failures are consistently highlighted...Until the public is prepared to accord social workers the status granted to others who have to perform difficult tasks for public benefit, some redress of public opprobrium is not out of place' (Kimberley Carlile, 1987, p. 7).

 Social workers are...employed to provide help, assistance, support and sympathy for their clients, and to promote and make possible change in even the most inevident people (Jasmine Beckford, 1985, p.202). Such a relationship involves attaining co-operation from the child or parent so that something positive can be achieved (Clare Haddon, 1980, 3.4.2 also Butler-Sloss, 1988, p. 27).

However, the social work role, as is explored in particular in the Beckford inquiry, is more than this. 'Social workers are also required by society to carry out certain duties and exercise powers, and these duties and powers are laid down in acts of parliament. These may require the social workers to implement decisions to go against the wishes of the client, and to exercise control if, in their professional judgement, the life and well being of a client — who may often be a child — is at risk. This dual mandate...imposes responsibilities for both social care and social control' (Jasmine Beckford, 1985, p. 202).

The Beckford inquiry contentiously notes that 'high risk' 'is not susceptible of definition', and suggests that 'rather than indulge in a massive reinvestment of resources, which at the optimum can minimize marginally the risk of injury, fatal or serious, to the child at home... society should sanction in high risk cases the removal from home of such children for appreciable time...It is on those children who are at risk — but where the risk is problematical — that Social Services should concentrate their efforts' (Jasmine Beckford, 1985, pp. 288–9).

A further complication is noted by the Doreen Aston inquiry. 'There is a popular feeling commonly expressed that children must be protected from danger. The simple fact is that under legislation existing in 1986 and 1987 children were not offered protection from danger. Social pressures have sometimes caused child welfare agencies to act as if they had those powers, but when they are exercised the same social pressures will say that the child should be protected from the danger of removal from parents' (Doreen Aston, 1989, 7.32).

MULTIPLE ROLES

One problem is the perception of the purpose of social work. The...Lucy Gates Chairman's report noted that in his view child care is specialist work and requires suitably trained field worker[s], yet there is a lack of clarity about training for what purpose. The inquiry notes social workers and health visitors attempt to understand the client and try to motivate change, and questions whether they were qualified to undertake what they appeared to be attempting 'this was work for the psychiatrist or a psychologist' (Lucy Gates, 1982a, 39.20)...

[The Beckford report asks] 'Can a social worker fulfil a policing role, firmly and efficiently, if he has also to gain the family's confidence, and to convey the personal warmth and the genuineness necessary for him to provide the support which will enable them to become better parents?'

'The duality of approach is by no means impossible to achieve, providing that the worker is clear about the nature of the job. It is essential that the worker recognizes that he owes allegiance to both the agency (and society) which requires him to be a child protector, and at the same time to the parent on whose trust he can build a relationship' (Jasmine Beckford, 1985, pp. 14-15).

The inquiry notes that 'Authority' is not a dirty word. Indeed, it must be brought officially from behind the arras of social work training onto the public stage, not just a child care law but also into the practice of all social workers. We regard this as an essential ingredient in any work designed to protect abused children' (Jasmine Beckford, 1985, p. 295).

(Department of Health, 1991, pp.4-5.) ■

Paradoxically, despite the stress each report placed on the difficulties faced by social workers, and the sympathy which their authors expressed this can also be seen to have undermined their professional position. In Cleveland, 'On the ground during the crisis, the social workers did their best under great pressure and in stressful conditions. The resources of manpower, skill and experience were inadequate to deal with the height of the crisis' (Butler-Sloss, 1988, p. 85). If their role is quite so difficult (virtually impossible) then it raises the question whether a new set of arrangements is required. This is apparent in the arguments developed within the Cleveland report and the way in which the evidence is present-ed. Although preliminary reference is made to the difficulties faced by the social services department, attention is quickly focused on the complaints of parents. In practice this means that the position of social workers is questioned consistently, without the report always having to do so directly. By utilizing a more judicial approach which sets out to accumu-late evidence incrementally the alternative professional ap-proach represented by social work is effectively undermined. The following extract from the report highlights some of the ways in which this was achieved. Here emphasis is placed on the ways in which parents felt themselves to be excluded from a decision-making process dominated by doctors and social workers. Using the language and complaints of parents, the report suggests that they were unable to influence what hap-pened. The retrospective judicial commentary contrasts with the immedi-ate pressures for decisions at the time:

■ RELATIONSHIPS WITH SOCIAL WORKERS

2.22   Social Services, inevitably perhaps because they were dealing directly with dissatisfied and unhappy parents, shared with the doctors the main thrust of the parents' complaints.

PLACE OF SAFETY ORDERS

2.23   A number of parents who gave evidence to the Inquiry referred to place of safety orders being used as a threat to achieve the wishes of the doctors or social workers. Some said that orders were unnecessary. Others complained of the timing or the method or circumstances in which orders were served.

DOORMAT

2.24   A father described a meeting with Dr Higgs and Dr Wyatt following the diagnosis of his daughter as having been sexually abused and his resistance to bringing his son to the hospital for examination. He said he was told he had no choice and went on:

'I was told that he may be placed in the care of the Local Authority if we did not have him examined'.

His wife told of returning to the hospital next morning and of Dr Wyatt saying:

'If you dare to take your child out of the hospital she will be placed straight into care'.

A place of safety order was obtained this day and the mother said:

'(that evening) I arrived home and opened the door to find a place of safety order on my doormat'.

PREGNANCY

2.25 In the case of a 3 year old girl, diagnosed by Dr Wyatt as being sexually abused, the mother was 17 weeks pregnant. The parents felt under pressure to accept the diagnosis in a conversation with social workers which touched on the wife's pregnancy. The father said that nothing was said directly but described asides between social workers as taking the form of:

'We want to get this sorted out before the next baby comes along' and he saw this and a similar statement made at the first hearing before the Magistrates' Court as implying that the expected child might be taken into care at birth. To another set of parents the matter was put specifically. Their two children had been taken into care and were subject of an interim care order when they received a letter from a social worker which referred to children she might have in the future and which included: '...there would be no guarantees from us that you would be entrusted to look after any child you may have'. The mother said she was pregnant at this time but as a consequence of receiving this letter the pregnancy was terminated.

BACK WITHIN THE HOUR

2.26 The parents of 2 children said that social workers were insensitive and unthinking when they walked into a hospital cubicle at 10.30 pm and, in the presence of their children aged 9 and 10 years, said they intended to obtain place of safety orders and 'would be back within the hour'.

BROWN ENVELOPE

2.27 The father of a 2 year old boy who had been diagnosed by Dr Higgs as sexually abused but who, with his parents' agreement, remained in hospital, told of being visited at ten minutes to midnight by two police officers and a social worker who served a place of safety order in respect of the child in hospital. In documentary evidence the parents of a year old daughter described returning to hospital to find a social worker waiting and being taken to the sister's office and given a brown envelope. They said the envelope contained a place of safety order and that the social worker simply and without explanation handed them the letter and left.

LYING IN WAIT

2.28   The parents of 3 children diagnosed as sexually abused, also told us:

'We were told place of safety orders would not be applied for as were leaving the children on the ward but when we got up the next morning at 8 am a social worker was waiting with orders outside our house.'

WELCOME ORDER

2.29   One mother expressed relief and gratitude to social workers for the taking of a place of safety order. She said that she approved of the taking of a place of safety order because her husband, the suspected perpetrator, had threatened to remove the child.

CASE CONFERENCES

2.36   Many parents felt strongly that they should be heard at case conferences. A number told the Inquiry that they were informed that case conferences were to be held. Some said they were told they could not attend. Others said they were informed they could attend but would not be admitted or would not be heard whilst the meeting was in progress. Some said they were told the results of case conferences. Others complained they were told neither of case conferences nor of decisions reached there.

NOT TOLD

2.37   A mother in evidence said she and her husband were not told that a case conference was to be held but that on a Monday she had a telephone call from a social worker telling her that a conference had been held the previous Friday. She said that when she asked why she and her husband hadn't been told of the case conference, the social worker said:

'they did not have to tell us if they did not want to'.

LITTLE SAID

2.38   In written evidence the father of three young girls, diagnosed as showing signs consistent with sexual abuse, in describing the parents' attendance at a case conference, wrote 'Came in at the end. Was informed about what the situation was — very little said. I complained at not being allowed in from beginning to put my point of view across'.

LETTER

2.39   The mother of a 1 year old girl told of being informed that she and her husband could attend the case conference but would only be permitted into the conference at its end when 'half the people would not be there.' She said that as a result she wrote a letter which the social worker told her was read out at the meeting.

NOT PERMITTED

2.40   Another mother said she asked if she and her husband could attend the first case conference concerning their child. She was told

/as not permitted but they could visit the Social Services office
 wards and would be told the result. She therefore wrote out the
 d's medical history and asked that it be put before the conference.
 e told the Inquiry she also asked for their general practitioner to be
 resent but learned later that the doctor was only informed on the
 morning of the conference and was thus unable to attend.

(Butler-Sloss, 1988, pp. 40–2) ■

The two main conclusions of the Cleveland inquiry have been developed
both in legislation — the Children Act 1989 (for England and Wales)
and guidance material stressing the need for social workers and others in
child protection cases to work 'in partnership' with parents (for example,
by ensuring their attendance at case conferences) and the importance of
inter-agency or multi-agency working. The key piece of guidance material
on child protection work is called *Working Together*. Although this is
explicitly subtitled a 'guide to arrangements for inter-agency co-operation
for the protection of children from abuse' it also begins by restating that
'local authorities must work in partnership with parents, seeking court
orders when compulsory action is indicated in the interests of the child
but only when this is better for the child than working with the parents
under voluntary arrangements' (Home Office et al., 1991, p. 1). Equivalent guidelines in Scotland (Scottish Office, 1989) were being redrafted in
the early 1990s.

These moves are likely to have fundamental implications for professional
practice and self-identity, although these are not always explicitly recognized. The stress on 'partnership' is intended to undermine professional
power as it has sometimes been understood. It is no longer the case (if it
ever was) that a professional expert (or group of experts) can determine
what is best and then ensure that it comes to pass. Instead plans have to
be negotiated both with parents and through the courts. Despite important differences between the position of mothers and fathers within families (for example, because most lone-parent families are headed by women
and most acts of child sexual abuse are perpetrated by fathers, step-
fathers or other men) the legislation refers to the collective 'parents'
throughout. Parents are said to have responsibilities to their children and
— as a consequence — effectively have legal rights to be involved in any
decisions about their future. Unless there is good evidence to the contrary
it is assumed that a child is better off remaining with her (or his) family.
The legislation also makes it easier for magistrates' courts to question the
recommendations of social workers and to suggest alternatives.

3.2 MOVING TOWARDS INTER-AGENCY WORKING

The growing stress on inter-agency cooperation changes the position of
professionals in rather a different way, since it implies, just as in the field
of community care, that no one agency (or, by implication, the profession
associated with it) is the sole possessor of necessary expertise in this area.

Instead the ability to negotiate with other agencies to produce consistent child care plans is more important than any specific social work expertise. Although it is not expressed in quite these terms, managerial rather than professional skills become more highly valued. Indeed in this context the existence of a range of professional skills each making claims to special expertise can itself be seen as a problem, if communication between agencies is made more difficult as a result. The Cleveland report placed great emphasis on this and suggested the setting up of special joint agency investigative teams to overcome it. Although these proposals are not developed in *Working Together*, as is apparent from the following extract, the stress placed on joint working is carried over, with a renewed emphasis on its institutional expression in Area Child Protection Committees (which take similar forms in Scotland and Northern Ireland):

■   Inter-disciplinary and inter-agency work is an essential process in the task of attempting to protect children from abuse.

1   Local systems for inter-agency co-operation have been set up throughout England and Wales. The experience gained by professionals in working and training together has succeeded in bringing about a greater mutual understanding of the roles of the various professions and agencies and a greater ability to combine their skills in the interest of abused children and their families.

2   Much has been achieved. However, co-operation and collaboration between different agencies is a difficult and complex process, particularly in an area of work like child protection in which policy and practice are constantly developing to absorb new ideas acquired through experience, research and innovative practice. All agencies concerned with the care of children are aware of the need to adapt and change in response to the growth of knowledge and understanding, and they must all share the responsibility for establishing and maintaining close working arrangements for all types of cases involving the protection of children.

3   For each agency, chief officers and authority members as appropriate must take responsibility for establishing and maintaining the inter-agency arrangements and should assure themselves from time to time that appropriate arrangements are in place. In the case of the National Health Service, this responsibility rests with the regional as well as the district authorities.

METHOD OF ACHIEVING JOINT POLICIES

4   In every local authority area there is a need for a close working relationship between social services departments, the police service, medical practitioners, community health workers, the education service and others who share a common aim to protect the child at risk. Co-operation at the individual case level needs to be supported by joint agency and management policies for child protection, consistent with

their policies and plans for related service provision. There needs to be a recognised joint forum for developing, monitoring and reviewing child protection policies. This forum is the Area Child Protection Committee (ACPC).

5   To be fully effective a joint forum needs to have clearly recognised relationship to the responsible agencies. Generally, one ACPC should cover one local authority and all the police or district health authorities or parts of them within that local authority boundary.

(Home Office et al., 1991, p.5.)   ■

The difficulties of inter-agency working should, however, not be underestimated. In the case of child protection work it implies the involvement of professional groups such as social workers (whether employed by social services departments or the National or the Royal Scottish Societies for the Prevention of Cruelty to Children), health visitors and doctors, teachers, probation officers and police. Each comes into the area with a different understanding of the issues and — possibly more important — with different responsibilities for what appears to be the same case (see for example, Hallett and Birchall, 1992, Chapter 7 for an effective review). The clearest tensions are probably between social workers, doctors and the police, each of whom has a different claim to expertise in the field.

Social work practice tends to focus on family relationships and the safety of the children within them. According to Dingwall (1986) an underlying principle is that the 'perceived autonomy of families should not be undermined (for example, by state intervention), except where families are clearly identified as having 'failed' in the socialization and nurturing of their children' (summarized in Horne, 1990, p. 98). Social workers 'are called upon to intervene in the balance between rights and responsibilities of family members when the behaviour of some may be harmful to others' (Hallett and Stevenson, 1980, p. 53). As we have seen, the Jasmine Beckford Report emphasized that social work had a dual mandate 'which imposes on social workers a responsibility for both social care and social control — the control work of the mandate being formalized by social work's statutory responsibilities' (Horne, 1990, p. 89).

Doctors have a particularly powerful role within the child protection process, because of the apparently objective nature of medical diagnosis, particularly in the identification of physical symptoms — which is in some way taken as the model for professional legitimation, dealing with 'hard' rather than 'soft' information as well as being able to provide 'cures' for individuals. Social workers often rely on paediatricians for expertise and evidence on health, physical and emotional abuse (see Stevenson, 1989a, p. 185). Department of Health and Social Security (now Department of Health) guidance for doctors reinforced this by emphasizing their role within the 'diagnosis' of sexual abuse, quite clearly remaining within the medical mode, although at the same time (in the wake of Cleveland) it seeks to stress the need for involvement with other professionals in the field, because 'it is unusual for the diagnosis to be made on physical signs alone' (DHSS, 1988, para. 5.2). Blyth and Milner (1990, p. 203) note 'that traditional training in medicine encourages the perception of the patient as the object of medical technique', which may mean that s/he is considered as a case whose problems can be solved, either by medical intervention (for example, setting a broken arm), or, in a parody of medical intervention, by isolation from the infection which may be defined as the family of which the child is a part. In court cases medical evidence of abuse is often still a determining factor of whether action is to be taken.

Yet, here another aspect of the professionalization of medicine may also become important. Doctors tend to value the mystique which surrounds their position. As Stevenson notes (1989b, pp. 185–6), their training encourages them to take an authoritative position on many issues which sometimes makes it difficult for them to accept an advisory rather than a decision-making role. On the other hand, the mystique surrounding their expertise means they are also often reluctant to make specific allegations or draw definite conclusions, because physical evidence can often be explained in a number of different ways, not all of which imply abuse. These points tend to hold for paediatricians as well as GPs, and psychiatrists are equally reluctant to draw firm conclusions in cases of emotional abuse. A further factor which needs to be understood as far as GPs are concerned is that child abuse is only a relatively small part of their work, much of which is defined in terms of providing health care to individuals and families. In some ways the identification of child abuse undermines basic sets of relationships and their identification of their own role, because it suggests that some apparently 'medical' problems cannot be resolved solely by medical intervention.

The role of the police also seems to be becoming more important. In the past the division between police work, concerned to assess whether sufficient evidence is available ('beyond a reasonable doubt') to convict an abuser, and social work, concerned to intervene on the less stringent criteria on a balance of probabilities to protect the child, has been relatively clear. But this division has become increasingly difficult to sustain, in part because the problem of child abuse has been recognized as more significant than had previously been believed so that criminal prosecutions in principle are seen as increasingly appropriate, and — paradoxically — because those accused of abuse frequently point to the lack of criminal prosecution as evidence to show that they are being unfairly victimized by social workers. In some cases the concern of police to identify criminal behaviour and the understandable tendency to lose interest if appropriate evidence is not forthcoming has helped to undermine the position of the social workers. In Cleveland the lack of cooperation from the police was one of the factors which the Butler-Sloss Report identified as a problem. There is a tendency for police to be sceptical about claims, or to seek evidence which is difficult to find (particularly since the evidence of children is easily challenged in court). Doctors have in the past played a major role in the child protection process, whilst also managing to be distant from it, and it now looks as if the police may be beginning to play a similar role. They, too, are able to import apparently 'harder' standards of evidence and investigation, which tend to undermine the 'softer' claims being made by social workers. The search for the 'truth' in terms of criminal procedure may interfere with the search for the 'truth' in terms of helping the child more therapeutically (see Hallett and Stevenson, 1980, p. 41). Research into police attitudes suggests that most ordinary police officers see the prime basis of cooperation between social services and the police as being the willingness of social workers to accept police 'common sense as the authoritative view' (Holdaway, 1986, p. 148).

By the early 1990s there was increased emphasis on the need for joint investigation with the police where child abuse was suspected (particularly in cases of sexual and physical abuse). This is clearest in England and Wales, where *Working Together* suggests there is a need for specialist investigation and assessment teams to be set up in both agencies to collaborate on this. In Scotland moves in this direction have been less extensively developed, not least because the Scottish Office has taken a less active part in issuing directives and guidelines (whether in the field of child protection or community care). The system of Children's Hearings which allow for a more informal yet legally competent discussion for child care plans with the involvement of parents and children may also work against the transfer of the more formal and legalistic system which currently dominates in England and Wales. But there are also problems with the Hearing system since it is based on the assumption that it is possible to get agreement between parties on most child care issues. That may not be the case with child abuse, since the abuser may attend and effectively intimidate the child. As a result there have been calls for change to allow children to be heard without parents present, as well as acceptance of the need for joint investigation with the police, despite its difficulties (Directors of Social Work in Scotland, 1992, pp. 39 and 46–7).

In England and Wales the Criminal Justice Act 1991 has made it difficult for social services departments to avoid joint investigation since although it allows the use of video-taped evidence from children in court, this also means that the rules of court procedure have to be brought back into social work practice, effectively limiting claims which might be made for more specifically social work expertise. According to the Memorandum of Good Practice on the use of video recorded interviews prepared by the Home Office and the Department of Health: *'The questioning by the police officers or social worker, in effect, replaces examination of the child by an advocate in open court*...joint investigating teams will need to develop a clear appreciation of the framework and rules of evidence in criminal cases. Their members are *not* expected to mimic advocates, but they will need to take proper account of the rules and the law in interviewing children' (Home Office and Department of Health, 1992, pp. 2–3).

It will be clear from this survey that there are genuine and important differences between agencies involved in the field. These differences cannot simply be wished away by the hopes of judges or management consultants. The dominant model of inter-agency working is clear enough. It implies a wide range of separate agencies coming together on particular cases, for example through case conferences, under the overall leadership of social services. But one of the consequences of inter-agency working is likely to be that negotiation between different professional and agency interests will dominate professional practice in the wider context of more tightly defined codes of practice allowing less scope for individual discretion.

In the context of inter-agency working it is difficult to sustain some of the wider claims made for social work (expressed, for example in Chapter 1). But, as suggested earlier, more specialist expertise called in to deal with particular problems may be given greater status, for example in the field of child abuse. Here, too, however, the nature of the expertise may be changing. Notions of treatment and therapy become less important as general bases of intervention: instead the language is that of protection and of managing cases or managing risk. The guiding principles are enshrined in law (for example, stressing the prime value to children of remaining with their families) and not traditional social work practice or professional training. As if to confirm this, the government rejected CCETSW's case for a three (rather than two) year social work qualification. Hallett contrasts the continued emphasis of the Children Act on specialist expertise and assessment with the looser notions of assessment associated with community care, and suggests two possible futures (Hallett, 1991 p. 289–90). In one there is a clear division between the two sides of social work and social services or social work departments, with the community care side effectively being defined as lower status and child protection (and child care) retaining a higher (and more professional) status. In some ways such an arrangement might look more like the old system — before Seebohm and Kilbrandon — but with the emphasis on specialist expertise in child protection and child care being still greater. The second possibility suggested by Hallett is rather different. Child protection work would no longer be able to justify its special position, somehow insulated from the arguments which already dominate in other areas of social work. Responsibilities might be divided between agencies with (child care) care managers preparing protection packages in much the same way as care managers working under community care legislation. Such possible futures for social work are discussed more fully in Chapter 6.

4 CONCLUSION: FORMS OF PROFESSIONAL SURVIVAL

Social work's claim to professional status lay in its identification with a generic skill. As we have seen, this is being challenged from above both by the development of community care and in the child protection field. Instead new sets of skills are being stressed, which focus on managerial and financial competences and on the ability to operate in inter-agency contexts or on specialist expertise in investigation and assessment. The wider professional claims of social work are increasingly challenged by the others who have some claim to their own area of expertise (in particular, for example, health professionals, doctors and the police).

The response of social work to these challenges has been twofold. The first has been forcibly to restate and extend the traditional values of social work, continuing to argue that it should have a major role in the contemporary world. This is apparent in the definition of social work used by CCETSW in its introduction to its rules and requirements for the Diploma in Social Work, which was quoted at the start of this chapter. It is worth reminding ourselves of the claims made in that definition:

> Social work is an accountable professional activity which enables individuals, families and groups to identify personal, social and environmental difficulties adversely affecting them. Social work enables them to manage these difficulties through supportive, rehabilitative, protective or corrective action. Social work promotes social welfare and responds to wider social needs promoting equal opportunities for every age, gender, sexual preference, class, disability, race, culture and creed. Social work has the responsibility to protect the vulnerable and exercise authority under statute. (CCETSW, 1991, p. 8)

The distance between a statement of this sort and the reality of most social work may be too obvious to need highlighting. But, to use the language of managerialism, it could be seen as representing a confident restatement of social work's mission tailored for the last decade of the twentieth century. As such it might provide a basis on which the profession could defend itself against the challenges we have been discussing, although some might feel that it faces the danger of leaving social workers unprepared for the world in which they now have to live.

The second set of responses have been rather different. They acknowledge the significance of the changes and seek to identify new possibilities within them. In the past, social work has tended to redefine itself to make survival (and expansion) possible. It initially grew in the interstices between other professions, with its main strength in hospitals and children's departments, with social workers only making more general claims to a wider role in the sympathetic political context of the late 1960s. There are signs that it is also learning to live in the changed environment of the 1990s. At a local level, social workers have had to change the focus of their work and have had to learn new skills. Trainers have been brought in to teach the new realities of managerialism, care management and budget holding. At the same time there has been a growth of specialist post-qualifying training courses. Many social workers have also sought to learn from the challenges from below which are discussed in the next chapter, seeking to define a new role for themselves. In a sense the real test of a profession is its ability to survive in a hostile environment. Social workers have proved able to adapt to previous shifts in the form of Britain's welfare state and their role within it, and they have stubbornly survived through the 1980s. They seem likely to do so into the next century, even if core features of their work change significantly.

REFERENCES

Audit Commission (1986) *Making a Reality of Community Care,* London, HMSO.

Audit Commission (1992) *The Community Revolution: Personal Social Services and Community Care*, London, HMSO.

Bacon, R. and Eltis, W. A. (1976) *Britain's Economic Problem: Too Few Producers*, London, Macmillan.

Barclay, P. (1982) *Social Workers: Their Role and Tasks*, London, National Institute for Social Work, Bedford Square Press.

Blyth, E. and Milner, J. (1990) 'The process of inter-agency work' in Violence against Children Study Group.

Boyson, R. (ed.) (1971) *Down with the Poor*, London, Churchill Press.

Brewer, C. and Lait, J. (1980) *Can Social Work Survive?*, London, Temple Smith.

Butler-Sloss, E. (1988) *Report of the Inquiry into Child Abuse in Cleveland 1987,* presented to the Secretary of State for Social Services by the Right Honourable Lord Butler-Sloss DBE, London, HMSO.

CCETSW (1991) *Rules and Requirements for the Diploma in Social Work. DipSW,* London, Central Council for Education and Training in Social Work.

Clarke, J. and Langan, M. (1993a) 'The British welfare state: foundation and modernization' in Cochrane, A. and Clarke, J. (eds).

Clarke, J. and Langan, M. (1993b) 'Restructuring welfare: the British welfare regime in the 1980s' in Cochrane, A. and Clarke, J. (eds).

Cochrane, A. (1993) 'The problem of poverty' in Dallos, R. and McLaughlin, E. (eds).

Cochrane, A. and Clarke, J. (eds) (1993) *Issues in Social Policy: Britain in International Context*, London, Sage.

DHSS (1988) *Working Together. A Guide to Arrangements for Inter-agency Co-operation for the Protection of Children from Abuse,* Department of Health and Social Security, London, HMSO.

Dallos, R. and Boswell, D. (1993) 'Mental Health' in Dallos, R. and McLaughlin, E.(eds).

Dallos, R. and McLaughlin, E. (eds) (1993) *Social Problems and the Family*, London, Sage.

Department of Health (1988) *Protecting Children: a Guide for Social Workers Undertaking a Comprehensive Assessment*, London, HMSO.

Department of Health (1991) *Child Abuse. A Study of Inquiry Reports 1980–1989*, London, HMSO.

Dingwall, R. (1986) 'The Jasmine Beckford Affair', *The Modern Law Review*, 49, pp. 489–507.

Directors of Social Work in Scotland (1992) *Child Protection Policy Practice and Procedure*, Edinburgh, HMSO.

Griffiths, Sir R. (1988) *Community Care: Agenda for Action. A Report to the Secretary of State for Social Services*, London, HMSO.

HMSO (1989) *Caring for People*, Cmnd. 849, London, HMSO.

Hallett, C. (1991) 'The Children Act 1989 and community care: comparisons and contrasts', *Policy and Politics,* 19, 4, pp. 283–91.

Hallett, C. and Birchall, E. (1992) *Co-ordination and Child Protection: A Review of the Literature*, Edinburgh, HMSO.

Hallett, C. and Stevenson, O. (1980) *Child Abuse: Aspects of Interprofessional Co-operation*, London, Allen and Unwin.

Holdaway, S. (1986) 'Police and social work relations — problems and possibilities', *British Journal of Social Work*, 162, pp. 137–60.

Home Office, Department of Health, Department of Education and Science, Welsh Office (1991) *Working Together Under the Children Act 1989. A Guide to Arrangements for Inter-Agency Co-operation for the Protection of Children from Abuse,* London, HMSO.

Home Office and Department of Health (1992) *Memorandum of Good Practice on Video Recorded Interviews with Child Witnesses in Criminal Proceedings*, London, HMSO.

Horne, M. (1990) 'Is it social work?' in Violence against Children Study Group.

Lait, J. (1981) 'Three issues for critics of social work training' in Anderson, D., Lait, J. and Marsland, D. (eds) *Breaking the Spell of the Welfare State. Strategies for Reducing Public Expenditure,* London, Social Affairs Unit.

Loney, M. (1986) *The Politics of Greed. The New Right and the Welfare State,* London, Pluto Press.

McLaughlin, E. and Muncie, J. (1993) 'Juvenile delinquency', in Dallos, R. and McLaughlin, E. (eds).

Nichols, G. (1991) 'Collaboration or conflict in community care planning: a health service perspective' in Allen, I. (ed.) *Health and Social Services. The New Partnership,* London, Policy Studies Institute.

Peitroni, M. (ed.) (1991) *Right or Privilege? Post-Qualifying training with Special Reference to Child Care,* London, Central Council for Education and Training in Social Work.

Russell, T. (1978) *The Tory Party. Its Policies, Divisions and Future,* Harmondsworth, Penguin.

Scottish Office (1989) *Effective Intervention: Guidance on Co-operation in Scotland*, Edinburgh, HMSO.

Saraga, E. (1993) 'Child Abuse', in Dallos, R. and Mc Laughlin, E. (eds).

Seldon, A. (1982) 'Introduction' in Parker, H., *The Moral Hazard of Social Insurance*, Research Monograph 37, London, Institute for Economic Affairs.

Social Services Inspectorate (1990) *Inspection of Child Protection Cases in Rochdale*, Manchester, Department of Health.

Stevenson, O. (ed.) (1989a) *Child Abuse. Public Policy and Professional Practice*, Brighton, Harvester Wheatsheaf.

Stevenson, O. (1989b) 'Multi-disciplinary work in child protection' in Stevenson (ed).

The Violence against Children Study Group (1990) *Taking Child Abuse Seriously*, London, Unwin Hyman.

Wood, N. (1991) 'Councils "should give up" social work role', *The Times*, 3 January.

LOCAL INQUIRY REPORTS

Doreen Aston (1989) Lambeth, Lewisham and Southwark Area Review Committee.

Jasmine Beckford (1985) London Borough of Brent and Brent Health Authority.

Kimberley Carlile (1987) London Borough of Greenwich and Greenwich Health Authority.

Lucy Gates (1982) Chairman's Report, London Borough of Bexley and Greenwich and Bexley Health Authority.

Claire Haddon (1980) City of Birmingham Social Services Department.

Liam Johnson (1989) Islington Area Child Protection Committee.

STUDY QUESTIONS

1   What were the main features of the 'challenges from the centre'?

2   In what ways has social work's relationship to the family been a major focus of these challenges?

3   What is the significance of ideas of 'partnership' in these challenges?

4   What are the implications of distinguishing between 'purchasers' and 'providers' for the provision of social services?

5   What are the likely consequences of these challenges for social work's future development?

CHAPTER 5
CHALLENGES FROM THE MARGINS

GEORGE TAYLOR

> Economic structures determine the roles of professionals as gatekeepers of scarce resources, legal structures determine their controlling functions as administrators of services, career structures determine their decisions about whose side they are actually on and cognitive structures determine their practice with individual disabled people who need help—otherwise, why would they be employed to help them?
>
> (Oliver, 1990, pp. 90-1)

Popular perceptions of social workers tend to be formed by their periodic appearances in the news media. And, whilst their activities are not always reported in a disparaging manner (Aldridge, 1990) it is always easier to recall the disasters and scandals; when, for example, it is reported that social workers have failed to take the appropriate action in time to protect a child from serious injury or death or, conversely, have removed children from their families, apparently unnecessarily, causing distress and hardship.

Social workers have always been subject to a range of legal, organizational, professional, social and emotional pressures and influences. As Rojek et al. describe it: 'The modern social worker labours in a climate of violent, unaccustomed, and changing uncertainties' (Rojek et al., 1988). Now, in the 1990s, they are also having to adapt to a major philosophical shift in their working arrangements. Social services departments, the vehicles for an unprecedented expansion of state social work provision in the 1970s, are now, following the cost-cutting exercises of the 1980s, either fitter and leaner or groaning under the strain, depending on your point of view. Against the backcloth of 'popular capitalism' promulgated by the Thatcher government, the discourse of state welfare is being rapidly replaced by the discourse of the market-place, and social services departments are establishing 'quality assurance' sections, and a tier of middle management whose primary responsibility is the purchase of cost-effective services. The notion of the social work 'client' is being replaced by that of the 'service user', and the operation of choice is being heralded as a guarantor of user satisfaction in the welfare market-place.

The expressed intention of these changes is to bring social workers into a closer working relationship with service users, more of a partnership than a professional-client relationship. How effective these changes will be remains open to debate and can only be accurately assessed after a significant period of implementation. To what extent they are commensurate with the wishes and aspirations of the people it is claimed they will benefit is a different question, and one that concerns us here. The legal and philosophical basis of social work is being changed by statute, ostensibly to the benefit of service users, and social workers are having to modify their approach so that they are able to 'work alongside' service users. But, as discussed in previous chapters, the activities of social workers have long been subject to challenges from user groups. Some of these challenges, such as that of the Family Rights Group, have highlighted the potentially oppressive nature of social work intervention. Such critics have claimed that the coercive power of the state has been brought to bear upon family life in a way that denies the civil and legal rights of parents.

To a certain extent some of these challenges have helped to shape the prescribed working practices of social workers, with the emphasis being placed on social workers reaching agreements with parents rather than assuming their parental rights. Other challenges cluster around the structural disadvantage experienced by certain groups in society, and their claim that social workers are instrumental in re-inscribing processes of oppression and inequality. Clearly, there are some fundamental objections to the nature and implementation of social work services that will be influential in shaping the future working arrangements of social workers, and present a challenge to the way they perform their duties.

In this chapter we will highlight some of these challenges. They are essentially of a 'personal as political' nature, in that they reflect on the relationship between the impact of social work upon the lives of service users and wider societal patterns and processes. An early example of this type of challenge is The Voice of the Child in Care, a London based group, established in the 1970s to enable children in care to articulate their experiences and influence social workers and policy makers. These have been replaced by the National Association of Young People in Care (NAYPIC) in England and Who Cares in Scotland. Another example is to be found in the growing number of political organizations for older people. They are known as 'Grey Power' movements in the USA, where such organizations have been established for some time, and they are beginning to develop in the UK around issues of poverty and disempowerment.

These challenges from the margins have a number of different voices, and we have chosen four examples to feature prominently in this chapter. They are: 'A chance for gay people' by Don Smart, in which he discusses the experiences of lesbians and gay men who wish to become adoptive parents; 'Toeing the white line', an article by Joseph Owusu-Bempah claiming that black social workers are being used to control the black community; 'Women confronting disability' by Jenny Morris, a challenge to the professional approach to disabled women; and 'Talking about a revolution', a feminist challenge to traditional social work by Liz Kelly, about the approach taken to child sexual abuse. The different voices articulate their own particular challenge to social work. They are not a unified opposition and they work at different levels. At times they are critical of the behaviour of social workers, at others the very nature of the social work task is challenged. This is an important distinction because whether social workers have had the 'professional' freedom to interpret their role liberally or have simply been following procedures has always been open to debate. As Allan Cochrane comments in the previous chapter, they are seen as either 'misguided do-gooders' or they are 'interfering and making things worse'. Under the Children Act 1989 and the NHS and Community Care Act 1990, the social work task is much more clearly prescribed and whether there will be much room for professional manoeuvre in the way that services are implemented remains to be seen.

The articles included in this chapter illustrate a set of challenges with which social workers should be familiar. Indeed, three of the articles have appeared in the social work press. It is not intended to undertake a sustained, in-depth, analysis of the issues raised, but to identify some common strands running through the challenges. A major aim of the chapter is to maintain that vein of accessibility, so that the issues under debate have a direct relevance to social work practice. In doing this we will highlight the underlying issues involved and, hopefully, avoid a simple criticism of social workers. Two of the voices (Don Smart and Jenny Morris) are of service users describing their own experiences. The other two (Joseph Owusu-Bempah and Liz Kelly) represent a more generalized criticism of social work and raise specific questions about the role of social workers in working with families. Whilst the challenges have their own particular focus, they are similar in that they have not been incorporated into the mainstream of social work thinking and practice and have been actively marginalized. They all raise questions about the way that social work constructs notions of family life, and it is possible to trace some common themes in the different voices, which present some difficult challenges for social workers. We shall use these themes to examine the extent to which the voices are being heard within social services departments.

5.1 DIVERSITY AND UNIVERSALISM

Shaped by universalist assumptions, social work has encountered challenges that it fails to respond to the diversity of its actual and potential client population. This has been particularly sharp around racial diversity and mono-cultural assumptions of social work theory and practice. Dominelli (1989) argues that the racist underpinnings of social work theory and practice mean that neither black nor white clients receive an appropriate service, and that white social workers fail to make the connection between racism and other forms of social divisions, such as sexism, ageism and classism. The origins of this mono-cultural view are deeply embedded in a British culture accustomed to being at the centre of a colonial structure, where it was seen as legitimate to export a British view of the world and impose it upon other cultures. As far as social work is concerned, the 'normalcy' of a universal view of social needs was reinforced by the Seebohm Report (1968). The idea of a single team structure located in the community and being able to meet all of its needs was, to a greater or lesser extent, translated into the subsequent setting up of social services departments. Jones (1983) argues that this was on a cost-benefit basis; that it is cheaper for social workers to help 'the poor' to become more self-reliant than face the prospect of an increasing demand for institutional alternatives or increased resources. The universalist assumptions that underpin such a strategy are significant for the way they deny the possibility of a structural causation of social problems and instead encourage individuals to fit in with what is held to be an appropriate and proper way of being in British society.

5.2 POWER AND RIGHTS

The traditional social worker-client relationship is an exercise in professional power — based, as it is, on an assumption that the social worker defines both the clients' needs and the means of meeting them. Individually and collectively clients have challenged this arrangement and claimed the right to define their own conditions. Such claims often involve critiques of the power of professionals in producing client dependency. An example of this is the way that members of the Deaf Community are beginning to assert their right to organize their own Community facilities, after more than a century of being almost completely dependent upon hearing people — the clergy, missioners and social workers being the primary influences — whose power they are now beginning to challenge. But the question of rights is not simply that of claiming something which is morally or legally yours. It is difficult, if not impossible, to disentangle questions of rights from questions of power. For rights are only realized if they are enforced and if there are sufficient resources to meet the demand. For example, the fact that under law all children of a certain age in Britain have a right to an education is meaningless if there are insufficient teachers being trained and employed. You cannot insist on your child receiving a particular standard of education if the local education authority has a shortage of teachers and is managing its resources as best it can. Likewise with welfare provision: the right to social services from the local authority does not mean you have a right to receive what you need, but that you will receive what the social worker recommends as long as it can be met from the organization's resources. The power imbalance in this equation is quite stark. The question of rights becomes subsumed within notions of professional judgement and financial management.

5.3 THE FAMILY

Families are a prime site for social work intervention and an increasing source of challenges to social workers. Working with families highlights another dimension in the social work debate about 'rights'. One area of conflict is that of identifying the client. This has been most visible in child protection work where the intersection of different rights (both legal and common sense) has shaped the patterns of intervention. Although the rights of the child appear to be foregrounded legally, claims on and against social work intervention have been made in the name of the rights of 'the family', the rights of the 'parents', and the rights of the mother and father (separately).

Social workers are also being challenged for making professional decisions based upon ideas about what counts as 'normal' family life. According to Janet Clarke of the Lesbian and Gay Foster and Adoptive Parents Network, 'there is still a prevalent notion of the "ideal" family being a married couple, and families outside of this are still seen to some extent as "deviant"' (Clarke, 1990). This is an issue highlighted by our first voice, 'A chance for gay people', by Don Smart.

5.4   A CHANCE FOR GAY PEOPLE

■ *Don Smart describes the difficulties he and his partner had as homosexuals when they set about trying to adopt a young boy with Down's syndrome.*

I believe that life is an art, and that the art of living can only be taken lightly by those who have been discouraged by their experiences. I have found a remarkable number of the latter working for social services, which is not a system I find sympathetic to the plight of the child. Children who are in need of fostering or adoption are often themselves discouraged.

Our experience goes back some time to the early seventies. We registered with a London agency for placing children with special needs for whom the normal avenues of support were closed. We found that as a male couple things were different and our story is referred to in Hedi Argent's book *Find Me a Family*.

Don Smart

When we moved to our present home fifteen years ago and, through a social work connection, my partner was put in touch with the single parent of a boy with Down's syndrome. The social worker felt she had devoted five years of her life to his welfare and training, and was now looking for a home to give him a wider experience of life and enable him to continue his schooling.

We were proposed and it was decided to give it a go, with the somewhat perplexed acknowledgement of the social worker, under the heading of private fostering.

The boy is now sixteen and has started college to continue his training: this despite repeated suggestions that his name be put down for Home Farm Trust. Possibly a sensible suggestion but not one that we thought in the child's best interests. Only the future will tell.

My partner tells the story of our subsequent dealings with a number of social services fostering and adoption departments in the following words:

> We thought it would be great to go into the nineties with our new boy whom we were hoping to adopt. We knew there would be problems, not only for the boy who had been in care for 11 years, but for us taking on the challenge.

> After 13 years of trying to adopt as a gay couple we were turned down again. People say that we would make good parents but we are not given the chance to try. How come?

> The last time we tried we were interviewed by a psychiatrist, which at first we did not mind. I later found out that hetero-couples would not have had to undergo this interview. I was very angry. Not wishing to give in I contacted five London boroughs to see what response I would get from them about fostering babies with HIV and AIDS. Either they didn't have a policy about working with lesbians and gay men, or they did not see that at present there was a need for such a service.

> As soon as they knew I was gay they tried to ring off. Many of these places have an equal opportunities policy but not when it comes to being gay.

This abbreviated account of our experiences gives a flavour of what it's like to be on the receiving end. The combination of clause 28 and the advent of AIDS propelled us both to involve ourselves in the issues.

On my part, it was from a desire to show society that it could always be different, a view I still hold. We see how badly people treat each other and we know what the stakes are. It is my belief that this century has shown mankind every consequence of its attitudes. If we don't like the responses we get then we can co-operate to change what we do. There is a lot more at stake than gay and lesbian fostering.

We found Dr Thomas Gordon's *Parent Effectiveness Training* the most valuable book on the subject of parenting and this has been our greatest encouragement so far. Moreover, it opened my eyes and ears to the mistaken methods that are commonly tolerated by biological parents, as though being a biological parent were a sufficient qualification for this complicated task.

I take the view that there are three main situations everyone must solve in life: the means of financial support; intimacy or sexual relationships; a social network and friends. If these are more or less solved it is possible to enjoy a 'normal' existence.

How we find the solutions is up to us and in no way do the solutions bear on parenting skills. Our own experience proves that this is so. Who needs to dissemble their sexuality? It seems unnecessary: all that is required is a willingness to co-operate and that surely is the aim of having an equal opportunities policy.

Judge not that ye be not judged.

(*Community Care*, 24 January 1991)   ■

The challenge presented in Smart's article goes right to the centre of a major difficulty for social workers: what is a family? The idea that families are the most appropriate place for children as they grow up is deeply embedded in the collective social work consciousness. This is hardly surprising as it is a central assumption of the wider social ideologies within which social work exists. But social workers are not merely bystanders in the arena of social organization. Some of them are employed specifically to be actively engaged in this area of work, and the discourse that underpins and shapes the management of children in care is that of 'substitute families', where social workers often work in 'family care' teams, whilst others are employed as 'family finders'.

What lesbians and gay men come up against when they wish to adopt or foster is that there is an unwritten central belief that a family should really be headed by 'a mum and a dad'. As far as adoption is concerned this has some legal basis, as under the Adoption Act 1976 only married couples or single people can apply for an adoption. One way around this for gay and lesbian couples is for one of them to make a single application to adopt, but this does mean that the child will have only one legal guardian and one of the adoptive parents will be without any legal rights at all. It is also likely that they would feel it necessary to conceal their sexuality to avoid prejudicing their application or, as Don Smart and John Elderton found, being subjected to extra vetting procedures such as a psychiatric interview.

The law concerning fostering (the Foster Children Act 1980) allows for a liberal interpretation by local authorities of whom they recruit and approve as foster carers. However, Clause 28 of the Local Government Act 1988 prohibits the promotion of the '…acceptability of homosexuality as a pretended family relationship'. The Department of Health's regulations on foster care state:

> It would be wrong arbitrarily to exclude any particular groups of people from consideration. But the chosen way of life of some adults may mean that they would not be able to provide a suitable environment for the care and nurture of a child. No one has a 'right' to be a foster parent. 'Equal rights' and 'gay rights' policies have no place in fostering services.
>
> (Department of Health, 1990)

The fragile nature of rights is clearly demonstrated by this statement when the power of government is brought to bear in a deliberate attempt to direct the actions of social services departments in the exercise of their professional judgements in relation to 'family finding'. As it transpired, the final sentence of that article was deleted from the final version of the guidance because it was considered by a number of child care organizations to be restrictive and unhelpful. Social services departments are acutely aware that if they actively recruit and approve gay and lesbian foster carers as part of their 'substitute family care' strategy, they may well be acting, if not illegally, then certainly contrary to the wishes of central government. Nevertheless, child care agencies have recognized that there may, at least, be 'special needs' which might make gay or lesbian foster carers an appropriate placement for a young person.

This presents social workers with a dilemma. Do they pursue the possibility of placing a child with lesbian or gay substitute parents in the knowledge that it will have to be justified at every stage, and in the end an adoption order is unlikely to be granted? Or do they pragmatically conclude that the child's best interests will be more effectively served by its being placed in a family that accords more with the expectations of social services senior managers, magistrates, and high court judges, who make the ultimate decisions?

A comprehensive assessment is seen as the cornerstone of all good social work practice, and in situations where the long-term future well-being of a child is concerned, social workers must consider a multiplicity of factors. What Smart and Elderton appear to be faced with is that their sexuality is of overriding importance as potential parents, and whatever else they may offer is barely taken into account. Pat Romans is an adoptive parent, an experienced foster carer, and a lesbian. Describing a research project into the lifestyles of forty-eight lesbian mothers, she comments:

> Being identified in terms of sexuality is a common experience of the lesbian mother. Social workers are seen to be guilty of this offence. One woman said, 'I was asked how many sexual partners I had had; I said it's not your business, how many have you had by the way?'
>
> (Romans, 1991, p. 14)

Romans claims that social workers are particularly powerful people in the lives of lesbian mothers, and generally demonstrate a personal hostility to the notion of lesbian parenthood. She reports that more than half of the women in the research sample practised some form of concealment of their sexuality, some even staying in heterosexual marriages, in order to '...avoid involving their children in its difficult repercussions'. According to Romans, the mother's desire to protect her children is used by social workers to control the lesbian mother, and even though relationships with individual social workers may, on the surface, be positive, the underlying philosophy of social work with its notions of 'normal' families militates against the acceptance of lesbian parenthood. This may create a dilemma for some social workers who may be sympathetic towards the notion of lesbian parenthood but consider themselves constrained by their professional mandate. The focus of power in this instance shifts away from the individuals directly involved towards the institutional control of social workers in the system, who in reality may have very few courses of action open to them. Romans challenges the rationale for much of the social work involvement with lesbian mothers and poses some questions for social workers engaged in such work:

> Is the situation a cause for concern and, if so, why? How much ignorance and homophobia is being allowed to influence decisions? Is there a need for social work intervention at all and, if so, to what purpose?
> (Romans, 1991, p. 15)

If Romans is right that lesbian mothers are being actively discriminated against by social workers, then the rights of lesbians and gay men to be considered as foster carers and adoptive parents are being infringed. The attack upon rights in this instance would appear to emerge from a number of different, but complementary, quarters. First, there is the public perception of gays and lesbians and their suitability, or rather lack of it, to be parents. Such a view is undoubtedly held by some social workers and is more than likely to influence their judgement. Secondly, there is the fact that there are certain legal restrictions placed upon gays and lesbians in the area of fostering and adoption. And thirdly, social services departments are clearly not adequately equipped and resourced to feel secure in undertaking work in this area and will, therefore, probably prefer to withdraw from it.

This does, then, raise the question about what happens in other areas of social work activity — for example, young people in care. As roughly 10 per cent of the population is either lesbian, gay or bisexual (Kinsey et al., 1948; Kinsey et al., 1953; Weinberg and Williams, 1974) we can expect this to be reflected in the 'in care' population and, therefore, it should be taken into account by social workers. But what is their experience of being cared for by social workers? The Albert Kennedy Trust was established in 1989, as a response to the perceived discrimination against young lesbian and gay people in care. Albert Kennedy was gay, and he frequently ran away during his eighteen months in the care of Salford Social Services Department. One week-end he fell to his death from a multistorey car park. The Trust named after him offers counselling for young gay and lesbian people and their parents/carers, a safe house to young people in crisis because of their sexuality, and respite care for lesbian and gay parents when ill. The Trust was founded by Cath Hall, who has experience of fostering lesbian and gay young people. According to Hall, many children find their way into the care system because they are struggling with their sexual identity and feel pressurized in school and social situations. In care the pressure is simply intensified:

> One young boy came to me when he was 16. He had been in care for three years. At his last place the other kids had urinated on his bed and torn up his possessions — they wrote gay bastard across the wall in lipstick. That's quite apart from the situation where the other kids refuse to share a room with them and staff find it difficult to do anything about it.
>
> (Hall, quoted in Sone, 1991, p. 12)

In establishing its pool of lesbian and gay carers, the Trust avoided calling them 'families', preferring to refer to them as 'big sisters or brothers'. Their rationale is not to do with legal prohibitions around lesbian or gay couples being seen as families, but a response to their observation that families are often places where young lesbian and gay people feel unhappy. The long-term aim is to have regional offices recruiting and approving their own carers working in cooperation with social services departments. It is easy to see why any busy social services department might welcome this development. Both the problem and the solution would be identified and addressed by a users' organization — offering mutual benefit within a spirit of cooperation.

Within this context, the issue of whether this initiative is helpful appears to be overshadowed by the way it challenges deeply held beliefs about children and families. The then director of Salford Social Services Department, Val Scerri, commented thus:

> I'm not sure how far the public and the council would find it acceptable for us to place teenagers with homosexuals. Our council members are looking to us to place young people in a normal environment — the element of risk a public body can take is limited.
>
> (Scerri, quoted in Bartlett, 1989, p. 7)

Social workers who are themselves gay or lesbian are placed in a terrible double bind by this kind of attitude. Do they avoid working with children and families altogether, or assist in implementing policies which impinge on their own way of life? Similar dilemmas, but to a much lesser degree, affect heterosexual social workers who adopt a liberal view of human sexuality. Because social workers operate both 'care' and 'control' functions, they are much less likely to take risks in areas where senior management, local politicians, and wider society hold strong views. Social workers are themselves increasingly the objects of management attention, and performance indicators, workload regulation, and regular appraisal exercises are being established as part of the local authority management systems. In this climate, with social workers feeling that their jobs may be under threat, the procedural-controlling functions of social work will probably prevail whilst attempts at advocacy, power sharing and risk-taking diminish.

The 'risk' of placing children with lesbian or gay carers is a complex of notions/beliefs/prejudices which require some unravelling if we are to understand their power. Male homosexuality has always been held to be a threat to the stability of Judaeo-Christian society, the penalty for which is death (Leviticus, 20:13). The medieval construct of male homosexuality was that it was outside of any communication with God and therefore located firmly with the devil. Homosexual acts were described as the 'abominable vice of buggery' in the 1533 Act of Henry VIII, punishable by death. The death penalty was imposed on 80 per cent of cases for homosexual acts in 1810, compared with 25 per cent for other capital offences. The 1855 Criminal Law Amendment Act (known as the Labouchere Amendment) extended the existing statute to make it an offence in private as well as public (Weeks, 1977). As Taylor and Meherali (1991) comment: 'The 1967 Sexual Offences Act loosened slightly the law regarding homosexual practice, by decriminalizing sexual acts in private between consenting men over the age of twenty-one. Surveillance continues in the public domain.' The advent of AIDS has, once again, linked the medieval notions of male homosexuality with sickness, ungodliness and death, precipitating another period of intense social pressure on gay men.

Another strand in this knot is the idea that lesbians and gay men are a bad influence on children: their sexual behaviour is deviant and they are unnaturally attracted towards children of their own sex. Consequently, they may encourage children into homosexuality or, at the very least, are incapable of providing appropriate role models. These fears ignore the overwhelming evidence that children are much more likely to be sexually abused by heterosexual men within their own homes (the Metropolitan Police figures indicate 96 per cent of reported sexual assaults on children are of this nature). Despite the intense social pressures to be heterosexual, 10 per cent of the population grow up differently anyway, so there is little substance to the claim that children brought up by lesbians or gay men would be unduly influenced in terms of their sexuality.

The 'facts' about lesbians and gay men, however, make little impact on the 'myths', for they are held on an ideological level, available to everyone and apparently based on common sense. Not only are they culturally embedded but they are also reinforced in statute. Social workers are also ordinary citizens and as susceptible to those ideas as anyone else, and this creates a tension in their role and presents them with a dilemma to be resolved. The social work task is not always clearly defined and social workers are subject to moral, legal and organizational imperatives, which may either conflict or concur with their personal politics when addressing these issues. Furthermore, the traditional base of social work, as discussed in Chapter 2, encourages social workers to identify and establish problems to be solved. The professional impetus to individualize and pathologize means that lesbians and gay men are likely to be understood in terms of the 'problems' they present to Western traditional notions of family life, what the Lord Chancellor, Lord Mackay, referred to as '…the basic building block of a free and democratic society…' (*New Law Journal*, 1989).

It is not surprising, therefore, that when it comes to recruiting lesbians and gay men as 'substitute families', or considering the needs of young gay people in care, social workers are struggling. The Children Act 1989 states that 'the needs and concerns of gay young men and women must also be recognized and approached sympathetically' (*Guidance and Regulations*, vol.3, Sec.9.50) and that 'preparation for this process should be incorporated in the care plan for the young person as soon as he starts to be looked after, accommodated or privately fostered' (Sec.9.43). This would appear to permit social services departments to address the needs of young lesbian and gay people at a structural level, but this would then bring them into conflict with the intentions of Clause 28, the restrictions of the Adoption Act, and the deeply held prejudices towards lesbians and gay men that exist within society. The challenge that social workers face is to what extent are they prepared to confront cultural assumptions and the constraints of statute, in balancing the needs of young gay and lesbian people in care and the rights of lesbians and gay men to be carers and parents, with the central focus that social workers have upon the idea that heterosexual families are the best places for children.

The idea that a particular construct of 'family' can be actively used to discriminate against a certain section of society is an issue that is also addressed in our second voice, that of Joseph Owusu-Bempah, the director of the Anti-Discrimination and Equal Opportunities Consultancy.

5.5   TOEING THE WHITE LINE

■ *Black social workers can unwittingly find themselves being used as agents of control in a dominant white society, according to Joseph Owusu-Bempah.*

Studies of prisoners-of-war have established that identification with the status and power of the captors is an important factor for the prisoners. They further seem to suggest that this identification phenomenon can also be observed at work in the process of socialization and professional training. For example, educational establishments and professional institutions, with their power or high social status, operate to change the layperson (such as a black person or a white working-class person) into a professional person — a lawyer, teacher or social worker.

Professional training affects the self-concept of the students: they designate themselves by an occupational self-reference, as teachers,

Joseph Owusu-Bempah

doctors, nurses, with increasing frequency as they pass through the various stages of professional training. The process also involves internalizing social and personality attributes deemed characteristic of the profession one aspires to, including even those which are not directly relevant. This is not very dissimilar to the 'identification with the captors' process.

The so-called helping professions, including teaching and social work are potentially insidious agents of social control. It is not surprising therefore that, like the police force, these professions are the ones which appear to be actively recruiting black people (presumably to control the black community). While not questioning the value of social control, what is of concern is the question of who controls whom, and to what end.

In Britain the dominant group (white people), via the various agents of social control, control minority groups (black people) in the interest of the former. The professions play an important role here. Almost every professional training in Britain is tailored to the needs and values of white people; it reflects and reinforces the exclusion of black people from all important spheres of life.

Set in a European framework, professional training 'pathologizes' or at best ignores black people's needs, values and culture, including even their family and kinship patterns. Black people are expected to conform to white middle-class needs and values in order to receive a professional service. Those unable or unwilling to do so are therefore pathologized by practitioners, such as teachers and social workers, who are ill-equipped by their Euro-centric training to understand or help them.

WHITE DEFINITIONS

Even the parental needs or circumstances of black people are defined by white institutions and their representatives. The West Indian family, for instance, is regarded as pathological on the assumption that it lacks a father whose role as guide and disciplinarian is assumed by white practitioners: magistrates, social workers, and teachers. Labelling the West Indian family as pathological enables representatives of the dominant group to encroach upon it for the purpose of control. Sadly, black people are increasingly being recruited in various capacities to perform such tasks.

This has far-reaching implications for black practitioners and their black clients. In their role as practitioners they are governed by white cultural norms and expectations which demand they regard their own culture as maladaptive. And given the insidious effects of the Euro-centric training and socialization on them, many may even regard themselves as the guardians of their clients, or community. That is, like the inmates of prisoner-of-war camps, they identify with powerful white institutions and professionals and try to steer their black clients — delinquents, offenders, patients, or families — to toe the 'white line'.

Many black teachers, for example, believe that the school is charged with the duty to instil white middle-class values into black (and white working-class) children to enable them to become middle-class themselves; losing sight of the adverse effects of racism on those children. Similarly it is not uncommon for black psychiatrists and psychiatric nurses to employ Western diagnostic tools to label black patients mad.

Nowadays it is almost sacrilegious to be associated with racism. White professionals are vulnerable in this respect. So to avoid being associated with racism, many organizations and professional bodies find it safer and more convenient to implicate further black people (victims of racism themselves) in racism by recruiting, training and employing them to implement racist policies and procedures on their behalf.

Measures needed to rectify this state of affairs should include the following:

- black students of the various professions need to take pride in themselves and their community;
- the training they receive should value them and their culture;
- while in post, they must be vigilant to ensure they are not used to do their employers' dirty work for them — to victimize or discriminate against black people;

- it is equally necessary for training institutions to embrace wholeheartedly the spirit of multiculturalism and equal opportunities, and incorporate it into their training programmes, by valuing and including the major ethnic minority groups and their cultures.

Until the European bias of professional training in Britain is remedied the black community will continue to be short-changed in their dealings with professional practitioners, irrespective of their colour or ethnic origins. (*Community Care*, 14 September 1989) ■

Many writers have commented upon the inappropriateness of social work services for the black communities in the United Kingdom based, as they are, upon a white middle-class model of service provision. Owusu-Bempah's challenge, however, goes further because it accuses the social work establishment of organizing itself in a way that deliberately discriminates against, and controls, black people. One of the mechanisms for achieving social control of black people, according to Owusu-Bempah, is the construct of black families promoted by white professionals. He cites the way the 'West Indian family' is viewed as pathological and, therefore, vulnerable to unnecessary oppressive social work intervention. Surinder Guru (1986), in arguing the case for an autonomous Asian women's refuge, makes a similar point. She claims that the social work establishment ignores the collective and political needs of Asian women who have suffered violence in their own homes and, instead, superimposes a stereotypical view of Asian women and their families in order to provide 'services'. 'In the main, groups for Asian women concentrate on childcare, keep-fit and English classes. Such preoccupations suggest that Asian women are ignorant and need to learn to look after themselves and their children' (Guru, 1986).

The pathological view of 'the Asian family', according to Guru, constructs it as a place where women and children are subject to strict controls, out of step with modern Western notions of family life and, therefore, legitimate targets for particular forms of social work intervention. The way in which Asian families are characterized differently from African-Caribbean families is interesting, in that it could be construed as a genuine attempt to respond to cultural difference.

This is a view that has some appeal to the dominant liberal-professional outlook in social work because it appears to pay some attention to positives — such as the inherent stability of Asian families — whilst, at the same time, relocating blame for difficult issues — such as the 'problem' of fatherless African-Caribbean families — to the broader shoulders of the state. On examination, it is a theory that is inevitably found wanting, as its major contribution is to place the Asian and the African-Caribbean communities of the United Kingdom in competition with each other as to which is making the best effort to integrate with British society and is, therefore, more deserving of state support. Errol Lawrence (1982) asserts that racist ideologies have adapted themselves to developing notions of cultural difference by, initially, recognizing the difference and then pointing out how the different communities present British (white) society with different sets of 'problems'. For example, the stability of the Asian family can be used to illustrate the relative disorganization of African-Caribbean families. But, as Surinder Guru has already demonstrated, in other debates Asian families are held to be repressive institutions for women and children. However, the relative autonomy of African-Caribbean women is not then seen as a positive feature of African-Caribbean families but rather as a problem. As Carby comments, the problem becomes '...the dominating Afro-Caribbean wife and mother, who is always out working and therefore never at home...' (Carby, 1982).

The inconsistency of the racial stereotyping here is marked, and somewhat contradictory. But is it haphazard or does it have some internal logic? Different forms of stereotyping are available for use at different times in support of the actions of professionals. The power of the discourse around racial stereotypes is that it is able to draw upon a range of sometimes contradictory statements depending upon the aims to be achieved. This selective use of particular accounts of the way that people behave is not peculiar to descriptions of black people. Potter and Wetherell (1987) point out that it is quite common to have a number of different ways of talking about someone, depending upon whether you like the person to whom you are talking and the purpose of the discussion. And that this use of language cannot be considered as simply neutral:

> ...the notion of construction emphasizes the potent, consequential nature of accounts. Much of social interaction is based around dealings with events and people which are experienced *only* in terms of specific linguistic versions. In a profound sense, accounts 'construct' reality.
>
> (Potter and Wetherell, 1987, p. 34)

In this case, the common-sense notions embedded in racist accounts of how black people in Britain behave, based increasingly in seemingly progressive understandings of cultural difference, construct a whole set of 'realities' about black people that legitimize forms of state intervention.

Sashi Sashidharan (1989) is in no doubt that a particular form of reality has been constructed for African-Caribbean people within the mental health system. Sashidharan comments on the over-representation of African-Caribbean people in mental hospitals diagnosed as schizophrenic — 50 per cent of all admissions compared with 20 per cent for white people. This diagnosis is then much more likely to be subsequently changed in the case of African-Caribbean patients than it is for white British, raising the question of whether the figures actually represent a predisposition amongst African-Caribbean people to develop schizophrenia, or problems with diagnosis. According to Sashidharan, black patients are often diagnosed as schizophrenic even when the 'core' symptoms are not present, and new categories of mental illness such as 'West Indian psychosis', 'ganja psychosis', and 'Rastaphrenia' have been invented, thus linking a

medical diagnosis of mental illness with racial origin and cultural practices. The recognition of 'difference' in this context is extremely negative
in that it assumes that there are inherent problems in belonging to particular racial groups. Sashidharan comments:

> The pathologisation of the black community, and of cultural differ-
> ences in particular, is taken a step further by the racialisation of
> schizophrenia that British psychiatry has achieved in its insti-
> tutional practice. This only leads to psychiatry being used, once
> again, as a powerful medium for articulating ideas about race —
> rather than about mental illness.
>
> (Sashidharan, 1989, p. 15)

According to Owusu-Bempah, social services departments are now
actively recruiting black social workers to implement racist policies and
control the black community. Certainly, there has been a marked increase
in the number of black staff appointed by social services departments in
recent years, and a number of new positions created for black staff to work
exclusively with the black community. This policy would appear to be
generated by a desire to offer appropriate services to the black community. But what is the experience of these workers within the local authority
structure? Gilroy (1987) suggests that 'Their perch in the institutions of
the local state is contradictory in both class and "race" terms'. He argues
that black social workers are essentially members of the professional and
managerial class whose job it is to perform local state functions with
people who are relatively poor and powerless. However, they can never
truly insulate themselves from 'race' politics. As Josie Durrant, the former assistant director of Lambeth Social Services Department, says:
'One's professional self stems from personal experience. As I once said to
my director: "I'm a black woman first and a manager is just a role that I
play. I can't stop being a black woman"' (quoted in Lunn, 1989, p. 23).

Durrant is critical of the impact that social work has upon the black
community, particularly African-Caribbean families who, she claims,
have been 'devastated' by social work practices. She indicts local authorities for mistreating their black staff, raising extra obstacles to their
promotion and expecting them to perform at a higher level than white
staff. And with a sentiment that ironically echoes that of the director of
Salford Social Services Department resisting the recruitment of lesbian
and gay foster carers, she is pessimistic about the speed of change:

> In any large bureaucracy change is enormously difficult to achieve
> particularly in respect of race. Local authorities don't encourage
> creativity. They encourage conformity. At the senior levels, despite
> what is said, creativity is not encouraged. You are expected to be a
> bureaucratic animal, worrying about budgets and elected members'
> agendas.
>
> (Lunn, pp. 24-5)

This would suggest that social workers working in the community are fairly powerless to effect change in this respect. The priorities of senior management focus upon maintaining the *status quo* rather than changing it, and as senior management teams in social services departments tend to be dominated by white, non-disabled heterosexual men, their views will inform and enforce policy. But whilst white social workers are not always aware of the racist nature of social services provision, black social workers are faced with it daily.

According to Gilroy, the stress of trying to manage contradictory notions of professional and cultural identity has resulted in black social workers espousing a 'black cultural nationalism', most conspicuously articulated around the issue of transracial fostering and adoption. The practice of placing black children in care with white families was relatively unknown before the mid 1960s, but has steadily increased since then (Small, 1986). The debate over the cultural propriety of such placements centres around the need for black children to develop a strong black identity which will keep them in contact with other black people and enable them to take a pride in their cultural origins. This in turn will help them resist racism by becoming more resilient and developing a healthy self-respect. Jocelyn Maxime (1986) argues that this is likely to be damaged if black children are brought up in white families. (See also **Dallos and Boswell, 1993**, for a discussion on the impact of racism on the mental health of black people in Britain). This way of thinking has gained some considerable ground in recent years and, whilst there will no doubt continue to be black children who are placed in white families, the Children Act 1989 states clearly that local authorities when placing children shall give due consideration to '...the child's religious persuasion, racial origin and cultural and linguistic background' (Sec. 22 (5) (c)). Of course, 'due consideration' is open to interpretation but there at least now exists a legal recognition, if not a general consensus, and it remains to be seen how this will be formulated into local policies within social services departments and translated into practice by individual social workers.

However, Gilroy argues that the effort put into the campaign for 'same race' placements by black social workers is a 'confused' response to the assertion that black families are pathologically disorganized and deficient. Born of the stress experienced by black social workers, a notion of 'black nationhood' has been constructed whereby black families and communities are respected, and only they can provide the appropriate environment for the rearing of black children. Gilroy argues that this is misplaced in Britain, where the black population is too small and fragmented to be considered as a homogeneous 'nation'. Further, he argues, the debates over 'race', culture and identity have been reduced to a single 'race'/colour issue, in which 'professionalized colour-matching' is of primary importance in the placement of black children. Within this paradigm the issues of why black children are taken into care initially are not addressed. Finally, Gilroy quotes David Devine (the chair of The Association of Black Social Workers and Allied Professionals) as saying, in a television interview, that the '...black community has been denied the right to look after its own'. This position, says Gilroy, is consistent with the philosophy of the radical right contained within the Thatcherite programmes of rolling back the welfare state and transferring the tasks of care to communities discussed in Chapter 4.

The implications of these debates and developments are profound for all social workers, black and white. At an organizational level they offer the prospect of 'change' within bureaucratic structures that seem designed to resist any form of significant change. At a personal/professional level, to the majority of (white) social workers they offer a series of dilemmas that cannot be ignored. In some ways the challenges have similarities with those that social workers face regarding homosexuality: deeply embedded cultural beliefs, organizational constraints, and inappropriate traditional professional modes of practice. But they also raise the question of *who* should be involved in social work with black people as much as the nature of the services. And at what level, if at all, is it appropriate for white social workers to engage with the issues? The employment of black social workers by itself has not led to major improvements. Indeed, Michael Hutchinson-Reis (1989) claims that '...there appears to be no fundamental change in the underlying racist nature of social work'. He points to the liberal-reformist underpinnings of social work as a negative force in enabling change generally, and in the case of black people it has served to define racism in a way that can be accommodated without too much upheaval to the system.

As new legislation, and changes to the structure of local government, begin to impact on social services departments, equal opportunities and 'positive action' policies will seem to be increasingly expensive within the welfare 'market-place'. Such changes are likely to affect the recruitment of black social workers to specially designated posts. In fact, the Government have recently announced that there will be no more funds for posts financed under Section 11 of the Local Government Act 1966, a major source of specialist provision for the black community. Clearly then, any debate about whether black people have a 'right' of access to a black social worker can have little impact at a practical level, as there exist very few ways of actively recruiting black people into social work. The reality is that, regardless of whether it is more appropriate for black service users to have a black social worker, there are too few black social workers, so the majority of black service users will, anyway, have a white social worker. There is insufficient account taken of the range and diversity of the users of social services, and the overriding factor is that of cost-effectiveness and efficiency of delivery. This way of organizing public sector responsibility constructs a view of social need that, in its narrowly defined form, can be matched by a traditionally based universal service provision. The effect of this is to shift any possibility of change to the already overburdened and ill-equipped shoulders of individual social workers, with the caveat that any attempt to step outside the constraints of official policy may bring them into conflict with their employers. Hutchinson-Reis offers them this advice:

I would ask that you respect the right of black colleagues to state their position separately. Do not feel threatened by this, but perhaps meet separately yourselves to discuss the issue of racism and what you can do to end it. Racism is an exploitive and oppressive system that you yourselves operate. This is not a reason to be overcome by guilt, followed by liberal good intentions. White social workers do have a positive part to play in combating racism, as well as other forms of oppression. To do this will require positive action. If you fail to do so, you may find yourselves marginal to profound developments in society.

(Hutchinson-Reis, 1989, p. 176)

The question of attitude is one that is taken up in our third voice, that of Jenny Morris, when she described the approach adopted towards her by professionals following an accident that resulted in a broken back:

5.6   WOMEN CONFRONTING DISABILITY

■ *Suddenly becoming disabled can be an earth-shattering experience. Jenny Morris recalls the shock she felt at how professionals treated her.*

More people then ever before are surviving spinal cord injury, partly because of better medical treatment following injury and partly because greater use of car seat belts and motor bike crash helmets means fewer deaths but more broken necks and backs. Therefore more and more social workers are working with those of us who are suddenly confronted with permanent disability.

I broke my back six years ago when I fell twenty feet onto a railway line while trying to rescue a neighbour's child. Among all the emotions I experienced during the following traumatic months, was a feeling of shock at the way health and social service professionals reacted to me. For example, the nurses in the general hospital behaved in an almost callous manner. It took a while before I realised they assumed I had fallen as the result of a suicide attempt and their automatic reaction to an attempted suicide was an unsympathetic one.

I was also shocked when the consultant at the general hospital to which I was admitted, decided without consulting me, that he would not refer me on to a spinal unit — 'for social reasons'. I had to impress on him very strongly that the fact my daughter was only one-year-old was not, in my opinion, reason enough to deny me the specialist treatment that I so desperately needed; he would not have assumed that it was so important for a man to stay in hospital close to home.

These two examples were just the beginning of an eye-opening experience in the way doctors, nurses and social workers brought their own preconceptions to my situation. There was little room for my reality in their assessments as to what action — or non-action — was required. I also found that feelings had little or no place in the

Jenny Morris

rehabilitation process. Or if they did, you were expected to conform to the professionals' ideas about how to grieve.

SHARING

In the weeks and months following my entry into the world of disability I desperately wanted to talk to other women who had been paralysed some years. And I wanted to read about their experiences.

When I left the spinal unit I found there were many other spinal cord injured women who felt the same. So in 1984 we organised two national women's conferences where, often for the first time, women shared their experiences of disability.

It was such a liberating experience, bringing out into the open our concerns, that we decided to write a book that would aim at sharing our experiences with each other and to impress our concerns on the professionals and the general public. We sent out questionnaires to all women members of the Spinal Injuries Association. Two hundred and five women responded, often writing pages and pages about themselves. *Able Lives: Women's Experience of Paralysis* (Women's Press, £5.95) is the result.

One of the clearest messages from the conferences and the returned questionnaires was how as spinally injured women our concerns are isolated within each individual's private world and were rarely made part of the public world. When we 'appear' as a public issue it is usually in the way the non-disabled world defines us and our concerns and not in the way we would wish to appear ourselves.

Our questionnaire covered all aspects of women's lives: not just the obvious ones of work, motherhood, and relationships but also those which are infrequently brought into the open, such as incontinence and pain. Women wrote, for example, about the effect of disability on sexuality. Few of us are given any help in confronting this issue. If we are lucky we are told the bare physiological facts that it is possible to have 'normal' intercourse (whatever that may be) and to bear a child following injury. Women wrote about how it feels never to have an orgasm again; how our sensuality changes; how incontinence affects making love; how our relationships have been affected.

One of the crucial aspects of women's lives before injury is that, if they are married or cohabiting, and particularly if they have children, they were usually the primary carers in their family after their injury and were rarely just the passive recipients of care themselves.

In spite of this, health and social service professionals often assume that, if we do not have a spouse or parent to care for us, then independent living is impossible. Single women in our study were at a higher risk of entering residential care than married or cohabiting women, regardless of the extent of paralysis or their age. This is a damning indictment of the philosophy of community care.

Most people following spinal cord injury have a great need for advice, expertise and resources from health and social services professionals. This applies not only when we are in hospital immediately after injury, but also over the years of disability, for our needs change. However, there are a number of barriers to getting the help we require.

There is rarely one person who can co-ordinate a response to all our practical problems (housing, money, aids and equipment, personal care, and so on). Instead there are a diverse number of services which seem to be in different places, with little interaction or communication with each other. If there was one person responsible for co-ordinating these different services our lives would be made a lot easier.

Another problem is the lack of specialist knowledge about physical disability among social workers in the community. This can cause particular difficulties for women who never get into spinal units (and this is a more common experience for women than for men) as it means they are unlikely ever to get access to specialist help from either medical or social services personnel.

ATTITUDES

Resource shortage is obviously one of the greatest but this is only part of the problem. More fundamentally, our experiences are determined by the reaction of the non-disabled world in general to disability. The dominant attitude is, on the one hand, to ignore the daily and detailed difficulties which we have, and on the other, to make heroes and heroines of those people who achieve some success in struggling against these difficulties. In these days of the celebration of the philosophy of 'every man for himself' such attitudes are extremely convenient.

Disabled people are perceived as being either 'wonderful' and 'marvellous' — or inadequate and unable to cope. Social workers often fall into this trap by explaining a lack of progress away by an individual's 'lack of motivation'. More generally, society can abdicate responsibility for collective provision as there is a mostly, but not entirely, unspoken belief that some people just cannot be helped because they are not 'survivors'.

It is this philosophy which makes the fight for the resources, to enable us to rebuild our lives, so hard. Disability itself does not determine the quality of our lives. Rather it is the resources available to us which make all the difference. If we have or can get the housing and personal care we need, if we have some friends and family who value us, occupations in and outside the home that we enjoy, then there will be joy in our lives.

We hope the experiences shared in *Able Lives* will go some way towards changing the attitudes of the general public and professionals alike. All of us, whether or not we are disabled, need a society which both cares for and values people, whatever their abilities.

(Community Care, 29 June 1989, pp. 14–15) ■

Morris's challenge to social workers is both general and specific. At a general level she is critical of the lack of specialist knowledge of physical disability amongst social workers, and also that professional notions of what it is to be disabled are given primacy over the life experiences of disabled people. The relationship between social workers and their disabled clients is conducted within a framework of 'provider-receiver', 'helper-helped', which locates social workers as powerful because they control the access to resources, and the disabled person as dependent. Michael Oliver (1990) points to the way that services are organized, and how they reinforce the dependency relationship because disabled people have little choice when, for example, it comes to *which* environmental aids they are given, or the *time* at which specific assistance, such as help with cooking or dressing, may be available.

Oliver also claims that the very nature of the professional-client relationship creates dependency and identifies the language that is used within these relationships to be important in maintaining the unequal power distribution. Changes in terminology away from 'client' to 'consumer', according to Oliver, acknowledge that a problem exists but do little to overcome it because the fundamental basis of the dependency is so widely and deeply rooted within professional structures.

The idea of breaking the dependency relationship, so that disabled people can move to a state of 'independence', is one that increasingly features prominently on the agendas of both social workers and disabled people. But Oliver is sceptical of the way it is being approached. The professional definition of independence, he argues, is based upon the disabled person acquiring practical daily living skills, such as self-care, whereas the disabled person's construction of independence is firmly rooted in their desire to be in control of their own lives. The two positions are not reconcilable because one depends upon the disabled person's response to the standards and assessment procedures of the professional, non-disabled, world, whilst the other is a state of mind and being that does not require 'able-bodiedness'. Morris makes this point when she refers to the way that disabled people who are considered to be making progress are 'wonderful' and 'marvellous', whereas those who do not measure up to the standards set by social workers 'lack motivation'.

Tracing the origins of this dilemma leads us back to the discussion in Chapter 2 of the 'psychology-complex' and the medical underpinnings of the development of social work practice. In this particular case, it is the development of the notion of rehabilitation that determined the course of events. On the face of it, rehabilitation is a good thing, as it enables someone who has lost part of their physical or mental functional ability to re-adapt to life in society. But, by focusing attention upon the disability, the process of rehabilitation also constructs a notion of 'normal', and that is: to be non-disabled. Within this context disabled people are viewed as deficient in comparison with non-disabled people. Dorothy Miles (1988) raises this point when referring to the struggle of the British Deaf community to have their language, British Sign Language (BSL) officially recognized. Despite the support of the European Parliament in 1988, and the fact that BSL is the fourth most commonly used native language of the United Kingdom (British Deaf Association, 1987), the central government view of Deaf people is that they are not a linguistic group. Translated into local government action, through social policies and grant aids, this view culminates in 'rehabilitation' being the overarching strategy for the organization of services for Deaf people. This professional construct of a Deaf person means that they, as Miles says, '...can only hope to become imperfect hearing people'.

The problem here is that if the service user holds a different view from the social workers of what should be happening, then negotiations may be tense and this could be interpreted by the social workers within the constraints of their working practices to the detriment of the service user. For example, in the field of child protection, an injury to a child may have more serious consequences if the parents cannot offer an explanation for the injury than if they admit to having caused it themselves. Whether the parents caused the injury or not, in one case they are seen to be remorseful and amenable, whilst in the other case it may be concluded that they 'lack motivation' to change and it is, therefore, not possible to work with them. Obviously there are fine judgements to be made in these cases, and the responsibility placed upon the social worker in attempting to assess the likelihood of future significant harm to a child is an onerous one. But it does also illustrate the dilemma faced by the service user — whether they be a parent, a child, a disabled person, or whoever — that working in partnership with the social worker does assume that the service user will accept the working practices and judgements of the social worker as being correct. The alternative is that the service user is viewed as someone who is either unable or unwilling to cooperate, and is therefore unlikely to gain access to services. The notion that there is a 'right' to services becomes transformed into a right to receive those services considered to be appropriate by service providers. And social workers, whose working practices are increasingly prescribed by statute and organizational procedures using a cost-benefit analysis of service provision, will inevitably relegate those service users who 'lack motivation' to a very low priority.

Morris's article also raises a specific challenge to social workers, and that is to become aware of the way that gender may structure the experience of disability. Fine and Asch (1985) argue that this has two major components: first, that disabled women cannot adequately fulfil an economically productive role, and second, that they are unsuitable for either producing or caring for children. The disadvantage that women experience in the job market is one strand of this problem. It is compounded by the concept of rehabilitation, because the emphasis is to help disabled people to become 'useful' and 'productive' citizens, a process which further discriminates against disabled women within a male-dominated society. The level of disadvantage increases when disabled women apply for social security payments, as eligibility for invalidity benefit depends upon previous National Insurance contributions, and the other benefit they can apply for, Severe Disability Allowance, is set at a much lower rate. Disabled women who are not eligible for either must apply for Income Support, but only if their income is below the poverty line (something that is all too easily achieved in these circumstances, and a theme which we will pick up again later). Lonsdale (1991) comments that there is a view that disability is much less traumatic for women, that they are naturally more passive and dependent. The disabled women in her survey, however, refute this idea, describing the loss of control over their lives when they became disabled, and expressing a strong desire for greater independence. Their experience of social workers had not been particularly positive as they, along with other professionals they encountered, were inclined to isolate the individual disabled woman from her social context, thus pathologizing the problem and creating a dependency relationship.

The other strand in the way that gender structures the experience of disability, according to Fine and Asch, is that of sexuality. Morris comments on the lack of any real information or support for the women in her survey. And a Thames Polytechnic report (1987) points to the 'urgent need' for improvement in the advice and counselling services about sexuality for spinal cord injured men. The implication is that sexual intimacy is not important in the lives of disabled people, but this is contrary to the findings in both the Thames Polytechnic report and the Morris survey. Latham (1990) claims that social workers have not developed an appropriate language with which to communicate with disabled people about sex, and he urges social workers to attend courses on 'speaking sexually'. Latham also refers to a survey he carried out in 1987 of public offices where disabled people might seek advice on such matters — only one out of twenty was fully accessible for those with a mobility disability. The following year a similar survey revealed five accessible out of twenty-seven. Access to public offices and the sexual needs of disabled people may not appear to be directly related, but this level of discrimination practically prevents disabled people from exercising any choice over who helps them with these issues and therefore maintains the network of unequal power relations. As Oliver pointed out earlier, it leaves the professional in control of whom to visit, in what circumstances, and at what time.

This is not to suggest that social workers revel in this state of affairs. Very few social workers would consider their working environment to be anything other than overcrowded and unsatisfactory and they are generally powerless to do anything about it. Similarly their access to further specialist training or funds to explore innovative ways of working is severely curtailed. Under the new working arrangements being brought about as a result of the implementation of the Children Act 1989 and the NHS and Community Care Act 1990, this situation is likely to worsen. This is particularly the case for social workers working with disabled people. As the pressure to use the private and voluntary sector to provide services for this group gathers pace the local authority social worker (as a purchaser of services) will be increasingly and significantly distanced from service users, and be less able to understand directly and therefore respond to the needs of disabled people.

The impact of the issues under discussion here upon the perceived and actual family life experience of disabled people is generally negative. Popular images of disabled people are simple stereotypes. Morris describes the social work view of disabled people as either 'marvellous' or 'inadequate', and Oliver comments: '...these cultural images have portrayed disabled people as less than or more than human and have been reinforced by professional conceptions of disability as adjustment to tragedy or the management of stigma' (Oliver, 1990).

The popular stereotype of disabled people and their families is that the disabled person is 'cared for' by his/her family. In an age when welfare is being rapidly de-institutionalized, it is likely that many more disabled people will be living with their families. But a general assumption that disabled people are dependent upon their families does not account for those disabled people who are, themselves, carers for families, or who live independent lives within a family structure, or who are children and would, therefore, be cared for anyway. The image of the disabled child is a compelling one (such as the dramatic pictures of disabled children in Romanian hospitals on the television news programmes throughout 1990) as it is the one most likely to invoke sympathy and, therefore, charitable donations. But the image of the disabled child also incorporates the essence of the stereotype of disabled people: that they are helpless and dependent. It could be argued that the professional view of disabled people attempts to maintain them in a child-like relationship with their families. The situation of the disabled adult being 'cared for' by an ageing parent is one that is all too familiar in social work, but it is not one that apparently engages social workers' interest. Wright and Alison, reporting on their study of older carers of disabled people in the UK, comment:

> In several parts of the country it had been made clear to carers that they could only ask local authority social workers for help in an emergency. Not only were these parents very uncertain about what constituted an emergency, they had a real need, like many older carers, for social work support and counselling about future living options.
>
> (Wright and Alison, 1991, p. 19)

Prior to the Industrial Revolution and the widespread establishment of asylums, most disabled people lived in their families and communities, fulfilling whatever role their capabilities allowed, similar to most other people. In the 1990s, the wholesale return of previously institutionalized disabled people to the community, under the guise of 'community care', cannot be construed in the same light. Under Western capitalism, society is increasingly self-regulating, with more closely focused definitions of what is 'normal' and what is not, and disability is consequently a much more stigmatized condition. Disabled people are marginal to the requirements of modern societies, and increasingly disadvantaged in the labour market. The reality for the majority of disabled people and their families is that of economic hardship:

> The Office of Population, Censuses and Surveys (OPCS) report 1989 showed that whether in work or out, these families were significantly poorer than average households, and that children with disabilities can look forward to a future of poverty if the figures continue. It states that 75 per cent of disabled adults in private households relied on state benefit as their main source of income.
>
> (MacDonald, 1991, pp. 9–10)

A number of writers (Jordan 1990; Becker and MacPherson 1988; and others) have commented on the fact that poverty is probably the most significant single characteristic of the clients of social workers. Which means, on this basis alone, the families of disabled people are more likely to have social work contact than not. Given the criticisms that have already been voiced regarding the nature of such contact, and the power that social workers have to grant access to services, it is reasonable to conclude that many families of disabled people are subjected to a form of intervention that they do not want and which fails to meet their needs. It is not a model of almost total exclusion, as is the case with lesbians and gay men, or of pathological inadequacy as with black families. It is a model based upon notions of deficit and dependency.

This is an important distinction to make because it illustrates the differences in the way that systems of oppression operate according to which group is being focused upon and the assumptions made by society about that group. For example: if we assume that the mechanisms of oppression (prejudice and discrimination) are fuelled by fear, then the fear that society has of homosexuals will be different from its fear of black people. In the former case it is the sexual dangerousness that is constructed around homosexuality that provides the rationale for the oppression of gay men and lesbians, whilst with black people it is a notion of racial superiority among whites and fears of cultural disruption that lends power to racism. In the case of disabled people the fear is not necessarily of them but what they represent. They are a reminder to non-disabled people that it is possible to join their group as a result of an accident or an illness. Able-bodied society tends to want to avoid contact with them if possible, and prefers that they attend their own clubs, and have 'special' working and living arrangements.

There is still the one approved way of being in British society: white, non-disabled, heterosexual, Christian, and preferably male, and the different marginalized groups each have a unique relationship with this monolith. The attitude adopted towards disabled people by wider society is patronizing rather than vindictive and means that disabled people are often the objects of charity, hence the proliferation of condescending projects such as 'Children in Need' and 'Red Nose Day'. Money may be raised to meet some of the needs of disabled people through these ventures but disabled people themselves are still left in a powerless position with no legal rights to the benefits acquired through charitable enterprise.

It has been argued that social workers view their disabled clients only in terms of their disability and, through their practice, encourage a dependent worker-client relationship. The family of the disabled person becomes permanently 'clientized', because the edges are blurred between the disabled person and their family as to who is the client, and this renders the whole family as a target for social work intervention. What families usually ask for is practical and financial assistance but the services they receive depend upon the social workers' assessment of what they need, and grants from charitable trusts depend upon an application from the social worker. In any case, money is rarely given. Grants generally take the form of a washing machine or cooker supplied from a specified store, or a holiday to be taken at particular resorts at a specified time. The element of choice is eroded and the process becomes institutionalized. The challenge facing social workers is to develop an understanding of the nature of disability within oppressive society, and to use the day-to-day experience of disabled people, in order to structure their practice.

Our final voice is that of Liz Kelly. This article is a report of the Feminist Coalition (Feminists Against Sexual Abuse). We have chosen it because it touches on many of the issues already discussed in this chapter, but more specifically because, in arguing the case for a feminist social work practice, Kelly links the issue of child sexual abuse with the 'problem' of male sexuality and locates it firmly within the orthodox family.

5.7   TALKING ABOUT A REVOLUTION

■   *In the week before the Cleveland Inquiry released the Butler-Sloss report, a Feminist Coalition (Feminists Against Child Sexual Abuse) issued a press statement and briefing document. The coalition includes individual women and groups from all over Britain and their goal was to claim a voice in the so-called 'Great Debate'. Their voice and their analysis was ignored. LIZ KELLY reports from the Coalition — setting the record straight.*

The document issued by the Feminist Coalition sets child sexual abuse in the context of a feminist analysis of sexual violence and raises many questions and concerns about the way the 'crisis' has been represented over the past year and about the likely outcome of the inquiry.

The public agenda agreed long ago by the media and the 'experts' excluded the most fundamental questions, the ones which feminists refuse to ignore or deny: who are the abusers, how common is child sexual abuse and why does it happen?

The agenda could have included a serious examination of the prevalence of child sexual abuse. It could have tackled the central issue of why the vast majority of abusers are male. Instead a media war was declared against a woman doctor and a woman social worker. These two women, committed to detecting child sexual abuse, have been 'found' guilty in order that 'nice, normal families' can be declared innocent. What will it take before the British press use banner headlines like 'Never again' about child sexual abuse, rather than its detection?

As a feminist I am pleased that the report did not add fuel to the scapegoating of Marietta Higgs and Sue Richardson, to the attempt to discredit professional women when there were individual men who played as much if not more, of a role in the 'crisis'. But the report raises many issues which as feminists we should be extremely concerned about. Three of these I wish to discuss here: the question of 'evidence'; the assumptions which underlay social work practice in Cleveland and which are central to the report itself; and the issues which the coalition accurately predicted would be ignored.

Unlike the Lord Chancellor, and some professionals, feminists know that there is no such thing as an 'infallible test'. We also know that the law has seldom been about either truth or justice when the issue is men's violence to women and children. Recent events in the US are a salutary reminder of the dangers of placing faith in the legal system. Judges are increasingly awarding access, and even custody, to men whom children have named as their abusers, and where often there was supporting medical evidence. An underground network, called the Sanctuary Movement, shelters and hides mothers and children on the run from court jurisdiction. Sanctuary are also supporting a growing number of mothers who as a result of refusing to tell courts where they have hidden their children are now in prison. In case anyone is foolish enough to think 'this couldn't happen here', the argument which justifies these decisions — that 65 per cent of children's accusations are false, and that false accusations are most common in disputes over custody and access appears without comment on page 205 of the Cleveland report! The male 'expert' who gave that 'evidence', also appeared recently on Channel 4's 'After Dark'. To anyone familiar with new research and practice in the US, it is nothing short of bizarre that this maverick's participation was sought in preference to internationally respected researchers or practitioners.

The starting point for feminists has always been, and must continue to be, the testimony of women and children. The coalition document quotes Lucy Berliner, an American feminist social worker, who has worked with children and women who have been sexually assaulted for 10 years:

> A legal decision should never be confused with the truth. If we believe what children say we will be right 95–99 per cent of the time, if we want signs and symptoms as proof we will be right 70–80 per cent of the time, if we require medical evidence we will be right 20 per cent of the time and if we have to wait for a witness we will be right 1 per cent of the time.

Reading the report with this in mind, and in the knowledge that what Marietta Higgs was trying to do was detect child sexual abuse early, rather than wait until children could bear it no longer and so told someone, some very interesting things jump out at you. Interesting things which the report itself glosses over and which the media have ignored completely, with the exception of Melanie Phillips' commentary in the *Guardian* on July 8th.

In no case was the disputed RAD (Reflex Anal Dilatation) test the sole basis for the doctors' diagnosis. Indeed the 'evidence' is there for all to see that for a considerable number of children a combination of factors, including the child telling before or after examination, VD, other physical signs or injuries to the genital area, the suspicion of adults based on the child's behaviour, existed. Furthermore, the cases where RAD played a more central role (according to Melanie Phillips 18 of 121 children) appear to be mainly those where siblings were examined after a brother or sister had been diagnosed as abused.

Cleveland's Director of Social Services, Mike Bishop, released figures on July 12th revealing that in 70 per cent of cases the cause for concern about sexual abuse was accepted by the courts — or by the families themselves. Claims that huge numbers of children were unnecessarily removed from their homes are simply untrue. In only 26 out of 118 cases (where children were made the subject of place of safety orders) did the law decide that the social services had 'got it wrong'. The 26 cases involved 12 families. Statutory court orders still cover 54 of the 118 children. The parents of a further 22 children have accepted supervision and support form social workers, in some cases because the abuser was someone outside the family. In 7 cases, children were sent home because the abuser was no longer living there — e.g. in prison. Finally, in 9 of the 118 cases 'We were suspicious of abuse...but could not prove it'. Mr Bishop pointed out that child abusers were often 'the best liars in the country'.

We know that most abusive men maintain their innocence to police, social workers and courts — why else do women and children have to give evidence, why else is it necessary to have medical evidence and other forms of corroboration to support their testimony? Yet the media ask us to believe these men simply because they anonymously deny the abuse in statements to the press or on camera. In case anyone feels this is a bit harsh, page 46 of the report contains a revealing account of how Stuart Bell (the Labour MP who played a major role in stimulating the media war) put pressure on a mother to join the parents' group, since he believed the man's denial. The mother, however, believed her child and had subsequently discovered that her ex-partner had a previous conviction for child sexual abuse! The reported rifts in the parents' group this week appear to be based on suspicions that some of the male members did in fact abuse their children.

Which brings me to the assumptions underlying the report itself and the reporting of the 'crisis'. Never do we read the words 'abusers' or 'men', let alone 'mothers' and 'fathers'. Instead 'parents' and 'families' are the focus. This is not accidental. It stems from a theoretical model which explains incest (it ignores other forms of child sexual abuse as it cannot account for them) as a symptom of a more fundamental problem: 'family dysfunction'. This model underpins, explicitly or implicitly, most professional practice in Britain and aspects of it have acquired the status of 'truth'[1]. It is this model which, as Mary MacLeod and Esther Saraga argued and the report confirms, determined practice in Cleveland. 'When Cleveland social services removed children from their families on place of safety orders they were not acting arbitrarily but following a theory... If it is the family rather than the abuser that is the cause of the problem then clearly the family cannot be trusted to care for the child'. It is not the 'management' of cases and the lack of trained 'experts' which is the problem, as the Cleveland inquiry suggests, but more fundamentally the way a particular understanding and explanation of incest determines professional practice.

What a feminist approach insists upon is distinguishing between the abusing part of the family (usually the adult male) and the non-abusing (usually the mother and other children). At once it becomes possible to think about how one deals with incest differently — remove the abuser and leave the child with the rest of her family. Justice Butler-Sloss herself notes (page 7) that this is 'the ideal' approach to investigation, but only touches on the possibilities of a different practice in an addendum to the recommendations on page 254. Would that judges felt ideals were worth fighting for!

Workers who act as if the family was the agent of abuse have already lost the possibility of building an alliance with the mother. Treating parents as a unity makes mothers feel responsible and blamed (which in terms of theory they are anyway). If a place of safety order is obtained for the children, the mother's only ally is the suspected abuser and her isolation enables him to convince her of the injustice since they are both 'innocent'. In order to work in a different way, we not only have to abandon the 'orthodoxy' in terms of theory, we also have to rid ourselves of the pernicious mother-blaming which abounds in this area (see the Cleveland report page 8 for some examples).

The strong version of mother-blaming is that mothers 'collude', the softer version which a number of feminists use is that they 'fail to protect'. Aside from the basic issue of whether adult women can protect themselves, let alone their children, from male aggression, there are important issues we need to explore here.

We have to distinguish between the minority of mothers who consistently refuse to believe their child, the even smaller number who did know and were unable to act, and the minuscule number of mothers who sexually abuse their children from the vastly greater numbers for whom the knowledge is, in the words of one mother 'the worst thing I could possibly imagine'. Building alliances with mothers means we have to imagine the worst. How would we feel to be told that a man we had chosen, trusted and probably loved, had abused our children? Wouldn't our first response be to wish it not to be true? Wouldn't we feel numb? Wouldn't we feel that our world had just fallen apart? Wouldn't we feel overwhelmed by a range of contradictory emotions: anger, fear, pain, sadness, guilt, despair, disgust? In order to work constructively with mothers, these understandable reactions must be validated, rather then interpreted as 'collusion'! With support, most mothers can work through their immediate feelings and are then able to believe and support their children. What is needed are not the specialist teams which Justice Butler-Sloss has put her faith in, but workers who are able to empower women and children and develop support networks within communities.

In our work we must also explore how abusers consciously entrap children and use a variety of strategies to convince them that their mother either cannot or will not believe or support them (note the similarity with how batterers isolate adult women from potential support). Some of the strategies they use are: telling the child her mother will not believe her; undermining the mother's authority; humiliating and/or abusing the mother in front of the child; and perhaps most effectively abusing the child in the mother's presence in such a way that whilst it is not necessarily apparent to the mother, the child thinks that the mother must know but is ignoring it. Seeing these planned strategies also helps us to understand the ambivalence and anger some child and adult survivors feel towards their mothers.

Whilst there are some legal routes by which abusers can be removed from the home[2], the experience of some areas in the US and a state wide initiative in New South Wales, Australia show that the most important factor in adopting this approach is to view incest as one form of child sexual assault, which in turn is a form of male violence. This enables a reframing of the issue, which when accompanied by funded community education can create a climate in which abusers are held accountable for their actions[3]. The crucial task for British feminists is to achieve this reframing.

There are a range of other issues which the coalition highlighted which both the report itself and the media response to it failed to address. They are summarized here as questions and issues which we need to discuss ourselves and take into the public arena:

- How do we counter the re-writing of history which is erasing the fact that it was the testimony of women survivors and the work of feminist groups which made child sexual abuse a public issue?

- How can we challenge the 'expert' take-over, which is transforming child sexual abuse from a political issue, about which feminists have much to offer in terms of theory and practice, into an issue about 'diagnosis', 'management' and 'treatment' which is the preserve of professionals?

- How do we develop an anti-racist practice which takes account of the possibilities that for Black and ethnic minority children the meaning they come to in order to explain the abuse to themselves, their possibilities to tell, and the implications of intervention may be different?

- How does disability affect the way children understand what has happened to them, their possibilities for telling and the willingness of adults to listen to them?

- What is 'prevention', since we know that telling children to 'just say no' is both inadequate and an inappropriate response?

If our voices are to be heard, if we are to have any chance of reframing the issues, we must talk and network with one another. The Coalition document provides one starting point. Feedback will be welcomed, as will ideas about how we can build a strong representative coalition, and what its priorities should be.

There are other starting points. It's not so long ago that reports like the one in *The Times* recently would have resulted in a storm of protest from feminists. When sentencing a 21 year old man to two years probation for 'unlawful sexual intercourse' with an 11 year old girl, the judge said 'In every other way you are an extremely nice young man. She was old for her years, you are young for yours, I can quite understand why you fell in love with her'. These days many women expect that others will respond and probably feel, like I do, both disappointed and guilty when another outrage passes without comment. Yet public protest has always been the most effective way of getting feminist analysis into the mainstream.

In the aftermath of Cleveland, we need to be clear that what we are seeking in the short-term is a revolution in the way child sexual abuse is understood and responded to. In the long-term our goal is a greater revolution which, amongst many other things, will make the question Tracy Chapman poses 'why is a woman (child) still not safe when she's in her home?' obsolete.

Notes

1   For a feminist critique of family dysfunction theory see: Carol Ann Hooper, 'Getting him off the hook — the theory and practice of mother-blaming, 1987, *Trouble and Strife*, No.12.

    Mary MacLeod and Esther Saraga, 'Challenging the orthodoxy: towards a feminist theory and practice', 1988, *Feminist Review*, No.28.

    Mary MacLeod and Esther Saraga, 'Against orthodoxy', 1988, *New Statesman and Society*, July.

    Mary MacLeod and Esther Saraga, 'Child sexual abuse: a feminist approach', 1987, *Spare Rib*, August, No.181.

2   For more details and discussion see: Elizabeth Woodcraft, 'Child abuse and the law', 1988, *Feminist Review*, No.28.

3   For more information on the New South Wales initiative see: Yvonne Roberts, 'It can happen here', 1988, *New Statesman and Society*, July.

(Spare Rib, No. 193, August 1988, pp. 8–11)   ■

The challenge that feminism poses to social work is broadly based and has an impact upon all areas of social work practice. Limitations of space do not enable us to address all of the issues involved here. (A more detailed account of a history of child abuse and the feminist position is undertaken by **Esther Saraga, 1993**). We are not suggesting that the article by Kelly represents the views of all feminist groups, but it does represent a strong challenge to social work in an area where social workers feel extremely vulnerable: that of child sexual abuse. And this particular challenge is constructed upon two themes that raise specific difficulties for social workers, the consequences of which we will examine here. They are:

1   In modern Western society the dominant construct of male sexuality is the major cause of child sexual abuse.

2   The nuclear family is an inequitable institution in which women and children are vulnerable to male violence.

Identifying male sexuality as a problem immediately confronts a number of weaknesses inherent in contemporary social work practice: most significantly, that social work has very few ways of 'dealing' with men. Saul Becker (1989) makes the point that social workers are much more likely to be working with female clients because social work is increasingly about working with people in poverty, and it is women who are expected to 'manage' the consequences of financial hardship. (This is reinforced by the increasing focus of social work on children and the general assumption that women have responsibility for child care.) Becker also claims that social workers help to sustain the systematic economic dependency experienced by women through their practice. By targeting the symptoms of poverty of individual women, and not addressing the structural inequalities, social workers are more likely to achieve some tangible evidence of change, but only at a personal level, and at the expense of any possibility of improvement of a substantive nature. Social work, according to Becker, has developed a contradictory approach towards the poor. Social workers are motivated by a desire to help, but they are also subject to social stereotypes of the poor as lazy, or as criminals. And, because 'they believe they can have little strategic impact on the structural nature of poverty', the needs and rights of women are suppressed within a framework of helping the individual (woman) cope with, and adapt to, her prevailing economic circumstances.

Bill Jordan refers to social work intervention as '...a series of transactions between deprived people who have lost control over parts of their lives, and social workers with limited resources but awesome powers to coerce' (1990, p. 164). And there is a parallel here with the challenge voiced by Joseph Owusu-Bempah regarding the employment of black social workers. Social work at a practice level is predominantly a female occupation and, as Becker points out, their clients are also mostly female. But the management structures of social services departments are overwhelmingly a male domain, so the policies that social workers (mostly female) implement are likely to be based in masculine values (even if problematized by feminist challenges) and therefore harmful to the well-being of female clients. Of course, this is a fairly stark way of articulating what is a very complex and difficult set of issues and, unless we wish to conclude that it is the result of a simple conspiracy, it is necessary to look further to see if there are other dimensions. The mechanisms of oppression that maintain the societal disadvantage of lesbians and gay men, black people, disabled people, and women are based on prejudice and power, and fuelled by fear. And 'fear' is a key concept in any discussion about the impact of masculinity on social work. As Vic Seidler comments:

As boys, we learn constantly to prove our masculinity. We can never take it for granted. This builds enormous tension into contemporary conceptions of masculinity. Fear is defined as an unacceptable emotion. But in disowning our fear and learning to put a brave face on the world we learn to despise all forms of weakness. We learn systematically to discount any feelings of fear and not to show our feelings to ourselves.

(Seidler, 1985, p. 155)

Given that social work is an activity mostly undertaken with the 'weaker' members of society, this raises a question not only about the disproportionate numbers of men in decision-making positions in social services departments, but their suitability for the social work task at any level. This is certainly an issue for male social workers in relation to investigations into child sexual abuse. Is it fair on the victim, after being assaulted by one male, to be confronted by a male social worker and asked to re-live the experience? If not, at which stage, if at all, is it appropriate for male social workers to become involved in sexual abuse cases? If we accept that the vast majority of sexual abuse is perpetrated by men (the feminist challenge), then for male social workers to withdraw from the scene would surely constitute a further abuse, through the expectation that female social workers will 'clean up the mess'. Furthermore, does it not simply serve to reinforce the notion that men are 'naturally' dangerous and prevent any possibilities for real change?

The social services' response to the developing awareness of the scale of child sexual abuse is mixed, although it is increasingly being organized around legalistic principles as, one after another, judicial enquiries criticize local authority procedures. Explanations of sexual abuse also reflect the diversity of the staff who work in social services departments, but this is unlikely to be translated into policy or practice because of the sensitivity of social services departments to public opinion. Senior managers in social services departments are not free to implement whatever policies they consider to be most appropriate. They must work in cooperation with elected council members, whose responsibility it is to represent the wishes of the local community. In the case of child sexual abuse, public opinion, as expressed through the media as well as local and national politicians, would indicate a great reluctance by society to take on board a feminist analysis of child sexual abuse that identifies male sexuality and family life as being major causes. A much less challenging, and therefore more acceptable, explanation is that of 'sick' families. That is, sexual abuse is caused by something 'going wrong' within the family, and therefore sexual abuse does not occur in 'normal' families. It is a notion that holds a central place in orthodox social work practice in this area of work, through the concept of the 'dysfunctional family' (**Saraga, 1993**). It has popular, political and organizational support, and it is consistent with the traditional base of social work which individualizes and pathologizes the nature of social problems.

Notions of family life have also been central to the major child sexual abuse cases of recent years: Cleveland, Rochdale, Orkney, and Nottingham. The idea that children had been removed from their parents without sufficient attention being paid to parents' rights was certainly a significant feature of the first three of those cases — Nottingham being the exception — and the public debate was constructed around the behaviour of professionals rather than issues of sexual abuse. The MP Stuart Bell talked about:

> ...a revolution that would swing power back to the parents and their families, that would check social services, that would make consultant paediatricians and their employers more accountable to the public, and would restore to government and Parliament a proper interest in family life.
>
> (Bell, 1988)

Events in Nottingham, however, took a different turn. Not only were there no criticisms of the conduct of social workers, they were actually praised by the Prime Minister for the way they handled the case. Thirteen adults, all from the same family, were charged, convicted and sentenced and the level of cooperation between the police and social services was high. That is, until information coming from the children in 'the family', via their foster carers and social workers, indicated that their experience was part of an organized 'ring' of wealthy men using their position and power to indulge in highly ritualized forms of child sexual abuse. According to Beatrix Campbell (1990), the police refused to act on the new information, saying that it did not constitute evidence of ritual abuse, and the director of Nottingham Social Services, David White, went on record as saying there was no such thing as ritual sexual abuse. (In a letter to *Marxism Today* in response to an article by Beatrix Campbell he later shifted his ground, saying '...it would be unwise not to accept the possibility that there were ritualistic elements to this case'.) A joint police and social services enquiry team discredited the work of the team of social workers, all female, involved in the case who, it was suggested by social services senior management, would need 're-training'. They were also threatened with disciplinary proceedings if they continued with their allegations, or if they discussed ritual sexual abuse in a public forum.

Amid the high profile elements of the case, such as the accusations that evangelical foster carers and social workers had encouraged the children to 'make up' stories of ritualistic abuse, the acrimony that developed between the police and social workers, and the ensuing crisis in the social services department, two aspects stand out. First, only immediate members of the abused children's family were ever charged, thus reinforcing the idea of a dysfunctional family. And, second, testimony by children will sometimes be accepted as 'evidence' and at other times not. The primary objective of the police in these matters appears to be to secure a successful prosecution, and the testimony of children will sometimes form part of the presentation of the case. Social workers, on the other hand, operate in a different reality and whilst to 'believe the child' and take action on a probability of events is often sufficient to satisfy the requirements of social services procedures, it sometimes founders on the hard rock of evidence demanded by the police and the courts.

The issue of children's rights is frequently lost in the machinery of professional procedures and criminal justice, and it is not surprising that there is a confusion about when social workers are providing a 'service' and when they are intervening on behalf of the state. The investigation of child sexual abuse brings this tension into sharp focus for social workers because of the nature of the event, the necessity to protect the child and the responsibility they have to assess 'risk'.

It is often unclear in the early stages of a child abuse investigation exactly what has occurred, and social workers have been criticized in these situations for removing children from their families precipitously. Social workers would argue that they were acting in the best interests of the child (i.e. to protect the child from further harm) and, despite the periodic public outcry against the actions of social workers, the legal position continues to be that the welfare of the child shall be given the paramount consideration.

A backlash from the Cleveland enquiry has led to a re-assertion of the idea of 'parental rights' but the extent to which these are entirely consistent with 'children's rights' is not always clear. Jordan refers to this as a 'no-go' area for officials:

> They are wanting to put a perimeter fence around something (the family's territory/property, or the performance of parental roles) so as to exclude social workers and others from any access, as critics, supervisors or protectors of children.
>
> (Jordan, 1990, p. 85)

Jordan identifies the Family Rights Group (FRG) as being one of the champions of this approach. And his analysis would appear accurate when you consider the FRG's submission in the *Inquiry Into Child Abuse in Cleveland* (FRG, 1988), in which they used the terms 'parent', 'family' and 'client' interchangeably, constructing the notion that any relationship between children and officialdom can only be conducted through their parents. It was made very clear in Chapter 12 of the *Cleveland Report* (HMSO, 1988), however, that '...the welfare and best interests of the child come first, even though this may conflict with the best interests of the parents'.

The feminist challenge, of course, locates the family as a place where women and children are at risk of being abused by men, rather than the safe and secure environment predicated by the supporters of parental rights. MacLeod and Saraga (1987) describe families as institutions where women are relatively powerless, and the opportunity is, therefore, afforded to men to sexually abuse children. Furniss (1991) is critical of this approach because it does not take into account the 'intergenerational' nature of the abuse — that is, it is predominantly a question of male adults abusing both boys and girls. He comments that the loss of this intergenerational perspective in the feminist approach means that the sexual abuse of children can be equated to the rape of women — another form of the abuse of male power. But Furniss argues that it is not helpful to see sexual abuse in this way because it ignores the fact that children are structurally dependent upon their abusers (unlike women, who, he argues, can liberate themselves from male violence) and that sexual abuse has a particular impact upon family dynamics. He describes the breakdown of generational boundaries, and an adult confusion between conflicts on an emotional and sexual level, as the cause of sexual abuse.

The extreme consequences of this, according to Furniss, are that '...boys may then grow up to become sexual abusers themselves and girls repeat the emotional-sexual confusion by becoming prostitutes'. This is not a new idea, of course: social workers are well aware of the idea of a 'cycle of abuse' and it is almost at the level of an accepted 'fact' that victims of sexual abuse are likely to become abusers. The evidence for this is very dubious, however, and the research must be treated with great care, as it is based on the life histories of known abusers, and does not take into account the unknown numbers of those people who have been sexually abused who do not become abusers themselves. Furniss' views place him firmly in the family dysfunction camp, and he is a strong believer in family therapy as the best means of responding to sexual abuse. In this he is closely aligned with what MacLeod and Saraga (1987) refer to as the 'orthodox' social work approach, which also sees 'family treatment' as the most appropriate intervention. Furthermore, Furniss identifies mothers as having a significant role in cases of sexual abuse, even when they are the non-abusing parent. Their position in the family means that they carry a responsibility for the quality of emotional relationships, and the way that sex is discussed, amongst family members. It is the breakdown of the emotional-sexual-intergenerational balance, according to Furniss, that creates the conditions in which sexual abuse will occur. Mothers are firmly implicated in this, either by entering into a 'collusion against any open acknowledgement of the abuse', or by helping to 'openly facilitate' the sexual abuse of her own children.

A criticism of this 'mother blaming' is a prominent feature of the feminist challenge to the family dysfunction model. MacLeod and Saraga argue that an assumption of the collusion of the mother is the starting point for therapy, and this characterizes both family and individual work in sexual abuse cases: 'A collusion *is* at work here: a collusion with a set of assumptions which allows families to remain exactly as they are, and which can have a ruinous effect on children and families' (MacLeod and Saraga, 1988).

A feminist analysis steps back from a construct of 'normal' family life, and rejects the notion of family dysfunction as being the cause of sexual abuse. The way that social workers operate in the area of sexual abuse comes in for the severest criticism because of, as Dominelli comments, '...the hurt-ful and damaging impact of the patriarchal assumptions embedded in traditional practice in both one-to-one work and family therapy' (Dominelli, 1987). But the implications of the feminist challenge are much wider than the issue of sexual abuse because, if the feminist analy-sis is relevant in that area, then the whole basis of traditional social work is fundamentally flawed by a failure to take account of gender relations in social work theory and practice.

5.8   CONCLUSION

We have concentrated, in this chapter, upon some of the challenges that social workers face around the work that they do with groups of people who may generally be considered to be their clients. These challenges are diverse and we have focused upon some particular themes that illustrate a number of dilemmas for social workers. That there is a gap between the senior management of social services departments and those people in receipt of their services is indisputable. The upper echelons of social services departments are overwhelmingly white, non-disabled, middle-class and male. Their 'clients' are usually not. It is also clear that, rather than being bridged, the distance between social services departments and service users is reinforced in practice, and that the combination of organizational procedures and traditional social work theory and practice simply serves to maintain the marginality of certain groups.

In the midst of this relationship between the local state and the individ-ual are social workers who are invested with institutional power based on legislation and accepted practice. By contrast, the rights of the service users are built upon shifting sands that require them to possess a lot of knowledge of the system, or be dependent upon the good will and commit-ment of their social worker. The notion of the client as service user is likely to perpetuate this situation because it is being pursued along tra-ditional social work lines of 'helping the individual to cope' — therefore denying power to the collective voice of marginalized groups.

The challenge that these marginalized groups present to social work is at its most critical when dealing with issues of family life. Traditional social work has a notion of family life at the centre of its operational strategy, and it is clear that this notion excludes lesbians and gay men, is deeply suspicious of black families and encourages dependency in the families of disabled people. Traditional social work is also deeply troubled by social theories that raise questions about accepted notions of sexuality and family life. This is most coherently demonstrated by the feminist chal-lenge to social work, which identifies traditional constructs of male sexu-ality and family life as a major cause of child sexual abuse and violent offences against women and children. But it is also raised by lesbians and gay men who claim that their sexuality is the focus of unnecessary atten-tion by social workers making judgements about their parenting abilities, and by disabled people in asserting their rights to be sexual beings, despite the lack of expertise amongst social workers in discussing such issues.

It is easy to be critical of social workers. They are, in effect, 'damned if they do and damned if they don't', and their shortcomings are often highlighted in the media. The reality for social workers, however, is that they operate in uncertain territory with scarce resources and very little public support and, despite this, there are many examples of good practice. But if the service to marginalized groups is to be improved, then the strands of inequality must be identified within the system. Whilst this will inevitably involve a restructuring of policy making, it is also necessary to examine the way that social workers conceptualize and implement their tasks.

A major difficulty here is that, whilst social workers are relatively power-ful in relation to service users, they are increasingly powerless within their own organizations, social services departments, which are them-selves being made more accountable for their actions. The split between 'purchaser' and 'provider' in the newly reorganizing social services departments means, as Allan Cochrane pointed out in Chapter 4, that the managers of care (the purchasers) are likely to have much higher pro-fessional status than the providers of care, but within a much more administrative regime. At the same time, the roles and responsibilities of social workers within the guidelines for child protection are being increas-ingly clarified and prescribed within a legal framework. The manner of implementation of these new working practices leaves little room for disagreement or debate, so overstretched individual social workers are in no position either to resist or modify their impact. As Bill Jordan com-ments:

> In an unjust society, social workers — like policemen and emergency service workers — have too many and too demanding responsi-bilities; they are not looking for more. The temptation is constantly to fall back into legalism, into a style of practice and ways of thinking...in which they stick to strictly-defined responsibilities, well-rehearsed procedures, and limited relationships as ways of dealing with complexity and overload.

(Jordan, 1990, p. 142)

REFERENCES

Aldridge, M. (1990) 'Social work and the media: a hopeless case?', *British Journal of Social Work*, 20, pp. 611–25.

Bartlett, N. (1989) 'Listening to the unheard voice', *Community Care*, no.780, 14 September.

Becker, S. (1989) 'Keeping a poor woman down', *Community Care*, no.746, 19 January.

Becker, S. and MacPherson, S. (eds) (1988) *Public Issues, Private Pain,: Poverty, Social Work and Social Policy*, London, Social Services Insight Books.

Bell, S. (1988) *When Salem Came to the Boro: The True Story of the Cleveland Child Abuse Crisis*, London, Pan Books.

British Deaf Association (1987) 'The case for BSL. BSL and Britain's minority languages', *The British Deaf News*, vol.18, no.9, September.

Butler-Sloss, E. (1988) *Report of the Inquiry into Child Abuse in Cleveland 1987*, presented to the Secretary of State for Social Services by the Right Honourable Lord Butler-Sloss DBE, London, HMSO.

Campbell, B. (1990) 'Seen but not heard', *Marxism Today*, November.

Carby, H. (1982) 'Schooling in Babylon' in Centre For Contemporary Cultural Studies (eds).

Centre for Contemporary Cultural Studies (eds) (1982) *The Empire Strikes Back*, London, Hutchinson

Clarke, J. (1990) 'Fit for a family', *Community Care,* no.808, 5 April.

Dallos, R. and Boswell, D. (1993) 'Mental Health' in Dallos, R. and McLaughlin, E. (eds).

Dallos, R. and McLaughlin, E (eds) (1993) *Social Problems and the Family*, London, Sage.

Dominelli, L. (1987) 'Family therapy is not feminist therapy', *Critical Social Policy*, Issue 20, vol.7, no.2, Autumn.

Dominelli, L. (1989) 'An uncaring profession? An examination of racism in social work', *New Community*, vol.15, no.3, April.

Family Rights Group (1988) *Child Sexual Abuse After Cleveland — Alternative Strategies*, London, Family Rights Group.

Fine, M. and Asch, A. (1985) 'Disabled women: sexism without the pedestal' in Deegan, M. and Brooks, N. (eds) *Women and Disability: The Double Handicap*, New Brunswick, Transaction Books.

Furniss, T. (1991) *The Multi-Professional Handbook of Child Sexual Abuse: Integrated Management, Therapy, and Legal Intervention*, London, Routledge.

Gilroy, P. (1987) *There Ain't No Black in the Union Jack*, London, Hutchinson.

Guru, S. (1986) 'An Asian women's refuge' in Ahmed, S., Cheetham, J., and Small, J. (eds) *Social Work with Black Children and Their Families*, London, B.T. Batsford Ltd.

HMSO, *The Adoption Act 1976,* London, HMSO.

HMSO, *The Foster Children Act 1980,* London, HMSO.

HMSO, *The Local Government Act 1988,* London, HMSO.

HMSO, *The Children Act 1989,* London, HMSO.

HMSO (1990) *The Department of Health, Foster Placement Guidance and Regulations, Consultation Paper Number 16*, London, HMSO.

HMSO (1991) *The Children Act 1989, Guidance and Regulations, Family Placements*, vol. 3, London, HMSO.

Hutchinson-Reis, M. (1989) 'And for those of us who are black? Black Politics in Social Work' in Langan, M. and Lee, P. (eds) *Radical Social Work Today*, London, Unwin Hyman.

Jones, C. (1983) *State Social Work and the Working Class*, London, Macmillan.

Jordan, W. (1990) *Social Work in an Unjust Society*, Hemel Hempstead, Harvester Wheatsheaf.

Kelly, E. (1988) 'Talking about a revolution', *Spare Rib*, no. 193, August.

Kinsey, A.C., Pomeroy, W.B. and Martin, C.E. (1948) *Sexual Behaviour in the Human Male*, Philadelphia and London, W.B. Saunders Company.

Kinsey, A.C., Pomeroy, W.B. and Martin, C.E. (1953) *Sexual Behaviour in the Human Female,* Philadephia and London, W.B. Saunders Company.

Latham, T. (1990) 'Taking the lid off the taboo', *Community Care*, no.800, 8 February.

Lawrence, E. (1982) 'In the abundance of water the fool is thirsty: sociology and black "pathology"' in Centre for Contemporary Cultural Studies (eds).

Lonsdale, S. (1991) 'Out of sight out of mind', *Community Care,* no.862, 9 May.

Lunn, T. (1989) 'Continuous agitation', *Community Care*, no. 771, 13 July.

MacDonald, S. (1991) *All Equal Under The Act? — A Practical Guide to Children Act 1989 for Social Workers*, London, Race Equality Unit.

MacLeod, M. and Saraga, E. (1987) 'Child sexual abuse: a feminist approach', *Spare Rib*, no.1, August.

MacLeod, M. and Saraga, E. (1988) 'Challenging the orthodoxy: towards a feminist theory and practice', *Feminist Review,* no.28, Spring.

Marxism Today, December 1990.

Maxime, J. (1986) 'Some psychological models of black self concept' in Ahmed, S., Cheetham, J. and Small, J. (eds) *Social Work with Black Children and Their Families*, London, B.T. Batsford Ltd.

Miles, D. (1988) *British Sign Language,* London, BBC Books.

Morris, J. (1989) 'Women confronting disability', *Community Care*, no. 769, 29 June.

New Law Journal, 14 April, 1989.

Oliver, M. (1990) *The Politics of Disablement*, Basingstoke, Macmillan.

Owusu-Bempah, J. (1989) 'The new institutional racism', *Community Care,* no. 780, 14 September.

Potter, J. and Wetherell, M. (1987) *Discourse and Social Psychology*, London, Sage.

Rack, P. (1982) *Race, Culture and Mental Disorder,* London, Tavistock.

Rojek, C., Peacock, G. and Collins, S. (1988) *Social Work and Received Ideas*, London, Routledge.

Romans, P. (1991) 'Women with much to offer', *Community Care*, no. 855, 14 March.

Sashidharan, S. (1989) 'Schizophrenic — or just black?', *Community Care*, no. 783, 5 October.

Saraga, E. (1993) 'The abuse of children' in Dallos, R. and McLaughlin, E. (eds).

Seebohm Report (1968) *Report of the Committee on Local Authority and Allied Personal Social Services*, Cmnd 3703, London, HMSO.

Seidler, V. (1985) 'Fear and intimacy' in Metcalf, A. and Humphries, M. (eds) *The Sexuality of Men*, London, Pluto Press.

Small, J. (1986) 'Transracial placements: conflicts and contradictions' in Ahmed, S., Cheetham, J. and Small, J. (eds) *Social Work with Black Children and Their Families*, London, B.T. Batsford Ltd.

Smart, D. (1991) 'A chance for gay people' *Community Care*, 24 January.

Sone, K. (1991) 'Outward Bound', *Community Care*, no. 875, 8 August.

Taylor, G. and Meherali, R. (1991) 'The other deaf community?', Unit 4 of *Issues in Deafness*, Milton Keynes, The Open University.

Thames Polytechnic (1987) *Personal and Social Implications of Spinal Cord Injury: A Retrospective Study*, London, Thames Polytechnic.

Weeks, J. (1977) *Coming Out*, London, Quartet Books.

Weinberg, M.S. and Williams, C.J. (1974) *Male Homosexuals: Their Problems and Adaptations*, Oxford, Oxford University Press.

Wright, F. and Alison, V. (1991) 'Still caring', *Community Care*, no. 877, 22 August.

STUDY QUESTIONS

1   Why is diversity a significant issue in challenges to social work?

2   In what ways is professional power a focus of such challenges?

3   What implications do these challenges have for social work's relationship with the family?

4   In what ways do challenges 'from the margins' differ from the challenges 'from the centre' discussed in Chapter 4?

5   What consequences are challenges likely to have for the future development of social work?

CHAPTER 6
NEW DIRECTIONS IN SOCIAL WORK

MARY LANGAN

> Twenty years after the Seebohm Report, social work has failed to establish its independent professional status, has a basic training shorter than that of other occupational groups involved in community care, and has dropped precipitately in public esteem. Its organisational future too is uncertain, threatened by the government's unremitting hostility to local government.
>
> (Bamford, 1990, p. ix)

It seems that social work has been in crisis for nearly as long as the British economy has been in decline. While Bamford questioned whether it had any future at all in the 1990s, Baldock summed up the plight of the social services in another gloomy survey of trends in welfare as 'a perpetual crisis of marginality' (Baldock, 1989, p. 23). Ever since local authority social services departments were set up in 1970, following the recommendations of the Seebohm Report, the personal social services in general and social workers in particular have come under hostile fire from left, right, centre and above all from the media. *Can social work survive?* was the menacing title of a vituperative attack on the fledgling profession launched from one new right think tank at the opening of the Thatcher decade (Brewer and Lait, 1980).

From the perspective of the early 1990s the answer to Brewer and Lait's provocative question is a qualified 'yes'. Social work has survived, but in a radically different form from that envisaged in the Seebohm Report. There were indeed dark moments in the eighties when even those most loyal to the profession confessed their doubts about its prospects. Writing in 1989, Bamford, for example, expressed the view that though social work might survive, social services departments were 'doomed' (Bamford, 1990, p. 166). Nevertheless, social services departments were identified as the 'lead agency' for the development of community care in the 1990 NHS and Community Care Act, despite the apparent hostility of Conservative Governments towards local government. Again, as one child abuse inquiry succeeded another in the eighties and social workers were alternately pilloried as 'wimps' or 'bullies', it seemed likely that responsibility for child protection would be removed from social services to some new agency. Yet the Children Act maintained the place of social workers in the expanding sphere of child protection.

However, though both social services departments and social workers survived, and were in a sense legitimated by the welfare legislation of the late eighties, they emerged in the 1990s with new roles and with circumscribed powers and prestige. The framework for both community care and child protection increased central government control and extended multi-agency collaboration on terms which inevitably reduced the authority of social services departments and the autonomy of social workers. The intrusion of surrogate or 'quasi'-markets and the new managerialism on the one hand, and the law and the courts on the other, imposed limitations on social workers' professional aspirations.

I   THE NEW MIXED ECONOMY OF WELFARE

The shift away from the post-war pattern of welfare services, in which the state played the central role, towards a new mixed economy of welfare, in which the private, voluntary and informal sectors play a much greater part, began under a Labour government in the late 1970s, but received its real impetus from the Conservative regime after 1979. The new framework was motivated above all by a concern to curb the burden of public expenditure on Britain's crisis stricken economy. It received ideological legitimation from the anti-welfare and pro-market outlook articulated by new right theorists and incorporated into the Conservative programme from the mid-1970s onwards. The restructuring of welfare was also profoundly influenced by the gradual subordination of local government — the key agency in the provision of personal social services — to central financial control and, ultimately, political direction, in the course of the 1980s.

The new mixed economy of welfare emerged in a gradual and piecemeal way in personal social services in the course of the 1980s. For a time social services departments were protected from the full impact of Government austerity measures by local authorities which cut housing and education budgets first. However, the combined effect of the continuing financial squeeze and measures to curtail the autonomy of local government resulted in a steady decline in the rate of growth throughout the 1980s. The practice of imposing cash limits led to underspending and undermined planning and innovation (Baldock,1989; NALGO, 1989). This sluggish growth in resources must also be set against the steady increase in demand resulting from demographic and economic trends and the increasing scale of child abuse, family breakdown, domestic and racial violence and the HIV/AIDS epidemic.

The first indication of a major government offensive on the personal social services came in a speech by health minister Norman Fowler in Buxton in 1984. In this speech Fowler first outlined the government's project of fostering an 'enabling' role for social services departments in planning, monitoring, supervising, regulating and supporting a range of private, voluntary and informal welfare services, rather than playing a major role as service providers. He also emphasized the need to use existing resources more efficiently and recommended attempts to attract resources from businesses, charities and voluntary groups. He proposed the more extensive use of charges (for services such as home helps and day centres) and the privatization of particular services (McCarthy, 1989).

In 1988 the Griffiths Report on community care outlined a comprehensive programme based on the application of the spirit of Buxton to local authority social services departments. It formed the basis for the 1990 NHS and Community Care Act. The Act's proposals (which were implemented in 1993) promised (or threatened) to transform fundamentally the mode of operation of social services departments and the practice of social work.

The Act declared an end to the social services department as a 'monopolistic provider' of services. In its place it launched an 'enabling authority' which would assess needs, design community care 'packages', secure service delivery and monitor costs and quality. At its centre was the split between 'purchaser' and 'provider' roles discussed in Chapter 4. Care managers, based in social services departments, would carry out individualized assessments of need and identify a 'package of care' to support the person in need. Care services would be purchased from within the mixed economy of care locally available: the range of public, private, voluntary and family based care providers. The legislation stressed two significant features to this process. First, it would be 'needs led', determined by the process of assessment of individual needs. Secondly, the 'client' would become a 'customer' — a purchaser of care services from within the mixed economy.

Both of these features are less clear cut than this sounds. Social workers and others have expressed doubts about the extent to which community care can be genuinely 'needs led' rather than 'resource limited'. At the time of writing, the Government has not established what level of funding will be available to support community care. In such circumstances, the concern that needs will be subordinated to resources in the management of care has become widespread. In relation to the view of the service users as 'customers', this is subject to a significant qualification. The service users will not be the direct 'purchasers' of services. Rather, their needs will be assessed and services purchased *on their behalf* by the care manager and social services department.

The new social services department is designed to promote 'cost effectiveness' and to encourage competition among providers, giving preference where possible to the voluntary and private sectors. The voluntary sector has steadily assumed much wider responsibilities in the social services field, as organizations like Age Concern, Mind and others now tender to supply services (Langan, 1990). The promotion of community care policies has meant placing greater reliance on informal carers, largely women in the family, to compensate for the decline in public and institutional provision for older people, people with mental illness, disabilities or learning difficulties, and children.

However, under the new welfare regime, the role of the state has not merely been cut back, but transformed. Market forces have become an internal organizing principle within the state sector. Like every other area of national and local government, social services departments have been subjected to reorganization according to managerial principles derived from the private sector (see Flynn, 1987). Throughout the new welfare state the rhetoric of delegated financial responsibility, devolved budgetary systems and localized cost centres now prevails. In the new internal markets patients, claimants and clients have given way to customers, contractors and users. Producers and providers are supposed to take second place to consumers and purchasers. Administrators and welfare professionals are now either subordinate to managers and accountants or have assimilated their skills and functions (see Clarke and Newman, 1993).

What are the consequences of this market-led restructuring of the social services department for social workers? On the one hand, social workers are moving towards a predominantly managerial role, as 'case managers' and 'care managers' rather than caseworkers or carers. Their responsibility is to assess needs and to plan and supervise the purchase and provision of appropriate care from a variety of agencies. The acquisition of managerial skills and qualifications could become a better guarantee of career advancement in social work than more conventional professional qualifications. On the other hand, the residual caring functions of social services departments are being devolved to social care workers, to workers in voluntary organizations, to 'volunteers', paid and unpaid, and to family, friends and neighbours. In the new mixed economy of welfare in social services, the local authority social services department remains the central planning and purchasing agency, but much of the work of providing care will be carried out by other agencies, by volunteers and family members.

As the purchaser/provider split is consolidated, social workers are increasingly likely to be found in managerial roles on the purchaser side, while providers, the new care workers, are likely to be workers in day centres, home care workers or even relatives. As critics have observed, this process is likely to result in a divergence between qualified social workers playing more narrowly defined professional and managerial roles, and less comprehensively trained staff carrying out practical caring tasks (Bamford, 1990; Langan,1992a). For Flynn, the future is one in which social workers will become 'a new breed of manager'. He emphasizes that they must become 'genuine managers', with a much greater 'political sophistication', rather than merely 'senior practitioners' qualified by greater experience or professional expertise in the theory and practice of social work (Flynn, 1987).

There are wide variations in the pace at which local authorities are drawing up community care plans and in the scale of local consultation. There are variations too in the extent to which other council departments, health authorities, family health service authorities, user groups and voluntary organizations are being involved. Not surprisingly, different models of community care are beginning to emerge with different implications for social work practice (see 'Inside the NHS and Community Care Act', *Community Care*, 28 March 1991). Some authorities are organizing social workers in intake and long-term care management teams based in particular districts. Others are pursuing neighbourhood based multi-disciplinary teams. Others still are establishing teams based on different client groups, with separate care management teams for children, people with disabilities and older people. However, whatever the specific form taken by the new community care arrangements, the break-up of the generic approach derived from Seebohm is the common theme.

We can see here the influence of the discussion around the Barclay Report with which we concluded Chapter 3. The neighbourhood team model follows the patch approach advocated by Brown, Hadley and White, while the client-specific teams reflect Pinker's specialist emphasis. The different approaches to organizing and delivering social work services developed in the Children Act and the NHS and Community Care Act underline the movement towards a more 'specialist' pattern. In this context, it is worth looking at the implications of the Children Act in more detail.

2   FROM CHILD CARE TO CHILD PROTECTION

> The policies and professional practices previously designated as child care, which formed the basis of the Children's Departments and formed a central plank of the Seebohm reforms of local authority social work in the early 1970s, have not just been redesignated, but have been reconstructed around the axis of child protection.
>
> (Parton, 1991, p. 203.)

As we have seen in Chapters 4 and 5 the challenge to social work over its long-established statutory responsibilities in relation to children has come from a number of different directions. Criticisms of the role of social workers have ranged from sober calls for reform from lawyers and academics to strident abuse from the media. The resulting contradictory sets of demands and proposals and the high level of public controversy surrounding issues of child abuse have caused widespread demoralization and confusion among social workers. Yet the 1989 Children Act has gone some way towards resolving these conflicting pressures through creating a new legislative framework and a clearer definition of the role of social work in child protection.

Social work with children has attracted controversy in three broad areas over the past two decades. Since the 1970s there has been growing concern about the sphere of *child care*, in particular about the evident increase in the number of children coming into council care and the growing proportion who have been removed from their families under *compulsory* rather than voluntary procedures. The wider use of 'parental rights resolutions', under which local authorities assumed full parental powers, and 'place of safety orders', used to enforce the immediate removal of children from their families were questioned by legal authorities, academic researchers and, not least, by organizations concerned about the rights of children and parents. In response to these concerns the Short Report [*Children in Care*] (Social Services Committee, 1984) and the subsequent *Review of Child Care Law* (Department of Health and Social Security, 1985) sought to shift the focus of social work from the statutory removal of children to a more professionalized model of good child care, emphasizing partnership, family support, maintaining links and the aim of returning children to their family of origin.

The issue of *child abuse*, which rarely left the headlines in the late 1980s, produced a contradictory set of pressures and demands, which Allan Cochrane has discussed in Chapter 4. A series of public inquiries into children killed by their parents while under some form of social services supervision provoked extensive and often sensational media coverage which blamed social workers and social services departments. Social workers were condemned as lacking in intelligence and common sense; they were pilloried as liberal and casual in their attitudes to child abuse; social services departments were targeted as callous, indifferent and unrepentant (Franklin and Parton, 1991). Strident editorials echoed judges and politicians in demanding a more authoritarian and interventionist approach to families in which children were at risk.

Social workers' response was to minimize the risk of child abuse (and their risk of being publicly pilloried) by resorting to a more conservative and defensive interpretation of their statutory mandate. The inevitable result was a sharp increase in the use of 'place of safety orders' in sharp contrast with the spirit of the Short report.

However, the revelation of alleged *child sexual abuse* on a large scale in Cleveland in 1987 and the subsequent removal of children from their homes provoked a quite different response and another conflicting set of demands on social workers. Some of these have been discussed by George Taylor in Chapter 5. The social worker was no longer a fool or a wimp, but a villain or a bully, a zealot and a bureaucrat, motivated by professional prejudice or feminist theory. Allegations of 'satanic' or 'ritual' abuse in Nottingham, Rochdale, the Orkneys and elsewhere in the late 1980s and early 1990s provoked similar responses. Now newspaper editors and politicians demanded more protection for children and parents against authoritarian and interventionist professionals. The official response to Cleveland, in the Butler-Sloss Report and the subsequent guidelines to concerned professionals, *Working Together*, tried to balance concerns about protecting children with the rights of parents. The law itself increasingly emerged as 'the crucial mechanism for decision-making and resolving disputes' (Parton, 1991, p. 114). Furthermore, the Cleveland report 'underlined the crucial need to legitimate and enhance the role and practices of social workers' (Parton, 1991, p. 115).

What was required was not merely to reconcile the tension between family autonomy and state intervention, but also to get the right balance 'between the power, discretion and responsibilities of the juridical, the social and the medical and their respective agencies and professional representatives' (Parton, 1991, p. 115). The 1989 Children Act set out to achieve this complex of objectives.

Given the extent to which social workers had become discredited in the public eye and disoriented by the contradictory tensions unleashed by the child abuse panic, some commentators envisaged that the tasks of child protection would be removed from social services departments and perhaps handed over to an agency like the NSPCC which already undertook extensive welfare work in this field. But the 1989 Children Act ratified the place of the social services department and social workers in child protection. It brought together in a comprehensive framework a wide range of pre-existing laws relating to child care and protection and sought to establish clear spheres of professional responsiblity and lines of accountability. The Act also revealed the Government's now familiar enthusiasm for extending the role of the mixed economy in the sphere of child care.

The main consequence of the extension of the *juridical* sphere into child care was the removal from social workers of some of the discretionary, rather paternalistic, powers they had exerted and, in the view of some authorities and parents, abused in the past. Under the new framework, social workers retained statutory powers, but were much more accountable to the courts. There was thus a shift from an ethos of professional paternalism and bureaucratic decision making to one influenced by the discourse of liberal individualism and juridically-sanctioned rights. Parton has identified a significant shift in the definition of the problem from a *socio-medical* one of *child abuse*, to the *socio-legal* conception of *child protection*.

Although the new law reduced social workers' powers *vis-à-vis* the courts, in a sense it also strengthened them *vis-à-vis* other professionals (and families) by giving the *social assessment* a key place in the identification of child abuse. 'Not only did social workers have the statutory mandate, but it was social knowledge which was crucial in constituting the nature of child abuse and the form that intervention should take. The social assessment was focal for identifying the high risk cases and thereby protecting children and the rights of parents' (Parton, 1991, p. 146). In this form, at least, there is a congruence with the proposals for community care which placed a high priority on the assessment of individual needs.

The Children Act thus endorsed the view that social workers had the professional skills required to 'interpret, construct and mediate the "subjective" realities of the children and adults with whom they work' (Parton, p. 115). These skills were vital in distinguishing — and, in the interests of not disrupting 'innocent' families, distinguishing correctly — between situations where intervention was necessary and those where it was not.

The theme of *dangerousness* was reflected in the Children Act's definition of risk of 'significant harm' as the criterion for invoking the statutory powers of the new 'emergency protection' or 'child assessment' order. This reflects a shift from the rehabilitative model of child care work in the

1960s and 1970s towards a more coercive model. The task of social workers is now that of carefully but rapidly distinguishing truly 'dangerous' families (which require intensive intervention) from not-so-dangerous families (which should be encouraged to carry on without social services interference).

At the same time the Children Act establishes a framework for providing supportive and preventive child care services for children *in need*. This involves a voluntary partnership between the family and the state in which the family acts as a consumer of a range of services, such as accommodation, day care and social work support. In the spirit of the new mixed economy of welfare these services are to be provided either directly by the state, or preferably by other agencies coordinated by the social services department.

Where the Community Care legislation sees an increase in the power of service users as something to be achieved through market mechanisms (the user as customer or, more accurately, 'quasi-customer'), the Children Act seeks to limit the power of social workers over clients by other means. In place of the market are legal and quasi-legal systems of appeal and complaint procedures, together with greater judicial scrutiny of social work decisions and processes. The Act is also notable for its stress on the welfare of the child as the governing principle in all decisions, although this may be tempered by the presumption that the family is the best place for children to develop. Equally significant is the requirement that all interventions must have regard for the child's 'race, religion, language and culture'. This gives legal status to both professional and user concerns that social work provision should become more attentive to the implications of multiple ethnic cultures (see Section 6.3 below).

Nevertheless, there are other concerns about the Act's consequences. Some critics have argued that the targeting of preventive services on families and children in need is too narrow, and marks the end of any lingering post-Seebohm ambition to see the state providing universal services. Others have pointed to how the Act's coercive features are statutory, while its preventive and service provision features are permissive. In a climate of limited public spending, such critics are concerned that social workers will find their efforts increasingly focused on the statutory obligations (especially child protection), while more general support services are neglected or decline (Langan, 1992a).

What does the Children Act mean for social services departments and social workers? In an important sense it has provided both with a significant role in relation to the biggest growth area in social services — child protection. This legitimation of the status of social workers is reflected in the trend towards the establishment of specialist teams of child protection social workers and in the emergence of advanced professional qualifications in work in this field. Yet this is neither a simple return to a pre-Seebohm golden age nor a great leap forward to a new child protection specialism. The Children Act has rescued both the social services department and social workers. But the new department is subject to the same mixed economy pressures of market forces and managerialism that we have discussed in relation to community care. The new professional status of child protection workers is circumscribed by the law and by the pressures of multi-agency working, not only with doctors, health visitors and family members, but especially with the police and the courts.

In another important sphere in which social workers have long-established statutory powers — that of mental health — there are striking parallels with trends in child care (Jones, 1988). Though issues of mental health have attracted much less public (and professional) discussion, similar criticisms have been made of social work practice in this area. In reflecting a shift from professional discretion to juridical control, the approach of the 1983 Mental Health Act has much in common with that of the Children Act in attempting to overcome them.

The role of social workers in the compulsory admission of people exhibiting signs of disturbed behaviour to mental hospitals came under increased criticism from a variety of sources from the 1960s onwards. Organizations upholding patients' rights and voluntary groups representing people with mental illness complained of the excessive use of statutory powers, of inconsistent and poor standards of practice and lack of communication with the individuals and families concerned. 'Anti-psychiatry' radicals questioned the role of social workers in colluding with the medical/psychiatric establishment — and often also the police and the courts — in incarcerating psychotic individuals in mental hospitals. In the 1980s groups concerned at the over-representation of people of Irish and Afro-Caribbean origin in British mental institutions questioned the disproportionate use of compulsory admission for minority ethnic communities.

The 1983 Mental Health Act attempted to respond to criticisms of autocratic and paternalistic behaviour by social workers in the mental health sphere. It ratified social workers' powers to secure compulsory hospital admission for those exhibiting seriously disturbed behaviour. However, these powers were subject to medical/psychiatric collaboration and to strict time limits defined in the legislation and supervised by the courts. The rights of patients and their families were codified and protected. Furthermore, to win the title of 'approved' under the terms of the 1983 Act, social workers were obliged to undertake a special course in mental health, a post-qualifying award of growing importance in social work today.

It is possible to see in these legislative changes a complex restructuring of the Seebohm model of personal social services provision. Three significant dimensions stand out. First, the break up of the local authority's role as the provider of generic social work services. The legislation has intensified tendencies to a greater professional specialization, and has separated the roles of assessment and management from the work of direct service provision. Local authority provided services will take their place as merely one segment of the new 'mixed economy of care'. Secondly, the changes are likely to create a substantial employment and career gap between qualified staff, mainly concentrated in the assessment and managerial tasks, and less or unqualified staff, concentrated in the varieties of service provider organizations. Thirdly, all the legislation highlights attempts to redress, at least rhetorically, the balance of power (and its implicit relationship of dependence) between the 'client' and the social worker. The main axes of this are the market/customer model in community care and the legal systems of scrutiny, appeal and complaint in child protection and mental health. In this respect, the changes have recognized some of the challenges from the margins to social work, although not necessarily in the forms that the challengers would have wished.

3   PRESSURES FROM BELOW

In the course of the past two decades social work has come under pressures from below as well as from above, from a range of user groups and pressure groups, as well as from radical movements both inside and outside the profession. The model users' group was provided by the Claimants Unions, which emerged in response to rising unemployment in the 1970s. This 'self-advocacy' approach, repudiating welfare paternalism as much as inadequate welfare provision, has been followed by tenants' organizations, pensioners, former mental hospital patients, alcoholics, drug abusers, women's groups and many others. Some of the key themes emerging from these movements have already been considered in Chapter 5.

At the same time, academics, politicians, welfare professionals and concerned individuals have sometimes got together to bring the needs of some neglected group to the attention of the welfare authorities. The Child Poverty Action Group, which was formed in 1965, has provided a model that has been followed by numerous organizations, from Shelter to ChildLine. As we have seen in the spheres of child care and mental health, the emergence of organizations upholding the rights of children, parents and patients have had a significant effect in publicizing grievances about social work practices, and their impact can undoubtedly be discerned in subsequent legislation. The influence of socialist, feminist and anti-racist movements, though less specific and more broadly focused than that of user and pressure groups, has been no less pervasive. Indeed many of the radical criticisms of social work have now been assimilated into the social services mainstream under the banner of 'anti-discriminatory' practice.

The radical social work movement, which we looked at in Chapter 3, was a more or less coherent force for reform within social services departments in the early 1970s. The journal *CaseCon* provided a forum for the expression of disaffection within social work and a loose organizational structure through which to challenge both the social services authorities and the emerging professional hierarchy. In circumstances of rising unemployment and growing austerity, radical social workers emphasized the structural determinants of deviant behaviour in society. They insisted that an analysis of the oppressive social relationships endured by clients was essential to understand their responses to society. Furthermore, the radical movement emphasized that the practice of social work as a means to correct clients' adjustment to an oppressive social reality was both futile and politically unjustifiable. Instead, they advocated a collective approach to the resolution of social problems, through working with tenants' groups, community associations, trades unions and other organizations of working-class people (Corrigan and Leonard, 1978; Bolger et al., 1981; Jones, 1983).

The fact that it was not until 1974 that the journal *CaseCon* published its first special issue on women reflected a central problem within radical social work. As a product of the established left, the radical social work movement was male dominated and often insensitive to some of the basic realities of the world of social work, notably the fact that the large majority of both clients and workers are women (see Brook and Davis, 1985). Inspired by the wider upsurge of the women's liberation movement in the course of the 1970s, feminist social workers drew attention to the role of patriarchal power relations in all spheres, from the families of clients to the hierarchy of the social services departments. They emphasized the need to raise awareness of these relations and to challenge them (Marchant and Wearing, 1986; Hanmer and Statham, 1988; Dominelli and McLeod, 1989; Hallet, 1989; Langan and Day, 1992).

Both radical and feminist social workers tended, in their early days, to neglect the specific needs and demands of black and minority ethnic communities. In parallel with broader trends in British society, social services have passed through three, overlapping, phases in their relations with black and minority ethnic communities. In the earliest, and arguably still the dominant, discourse the object of the majority ethnic community is to *assimilate* those of a different racial or ethnic origin. From this perspective it is up to black and minority ethnic people to integrate with the majority and accept its cultural norms and values as their own: 'special treatment' is out. In the sphere of social services, this approach led to the 'colour-blind' policy towards fostering and adoption. This resulted in black children being routinely placed with white families, as though their ethnic identity was of no particular importance.

In the 1970s the growing recognition of the refusal of black and minority ethnic peoples to abandon their identities led to a shift towards a *multicultural* perspective. This accepted the inevitability of diverse identities and recognized the special needs of minorities, particularly in the spheres of education, housing and employment. The 1976 Race Relations Act for the first time gave local authorities statutory duties to eliminate unlawful racial discrimination and to promote equal opportunities and good race relations. However, in 1978 a survey conducted jointly by the Association of Directors of Social Services and the Commission for Racial Equality noted that the social services response to multi-racial communities was 'patchy, piecemeal and lacking in strategy' (Connelly, 1990, p. 64).

In the early 1980s the multi-cultural approach received a major boost from the election of a number of left-led Labour councils in key urban areas, often including for the first time prominent representatives of the black and minority ethnic communities. Such councils proclaimed bold equal opportunities policies and created measures to raise awareness of racial inequalities. One consequence of this new outlook was the shift away from trans-racial fostering and adoption, and the active recruitment of black alternative families for black children in council care. Another consequence was the growing recognition of the over-representation of black people in the 'control' spheres of social services provision, as targets of child protection interventions and compulsory admission to mental hospitals, and their under-representation in 'caring' spheres, such as day centres and home care schemes (Roys, 1988, p. 210). The first steps towards opening access to social work courses and career opportunities to black and minority ethnic applicants were part of the social services' acknowledgement of these 'problems'.

However, the very promotion of Britain as a multi-cultural society only drew attention to the dominance of one culture over all others. It appeared to many that the multi-culturalist approach was failing to overcome the obstacles facing black people because it ignored the effects of racism. A few councils moved beyond multi-culturalism to promote an *anti-racist* approach (Ball et al., 1990). They emphasized the pervasive structures of discrimination against black people in British society and the need to confront them through positive action, in employment, education and social services. Anti-racism attracted much hostile reaction, both from central government and the mass media, and was, in the process, equated with 'loony left' local councils.

The immediate result was a retreat from the anti-racist approach. While most councils maintained formal equal opportunities policies, some went further and sacked race relations advisors and abandoned multi-culturalist policies. Noting that 'today the scene is one of confusion and acrimony', one commentator has concluded that 'the local politics of race has become polarized around a more intense espousal of race-specific measures on the one hand and their more dismissive disavowal on the other' (Young, 1990, p. 30).

The movement towards anti-discriminatory social work took off from the anti-racist critique of all aspects of social services theory and practice in the 1980s. It broadened out through the inclusion of the critiques of members of different ethnic, national, religious and cultural identities as well as those of lesbians and gay men, people with disabilities and older men and women. From within the women's movement, the autonomous organizations of black people and those of other groups came further demands that the world of social work acknowledge the diversity of oppression in British society and organize to tackle it (Langan and Lee, 1989).

The attempt to construct an anti-discriminatory social work has taken shape out of a growing recognition of the specificities of oppression according to gender, race, class, age, disability and sexual orientation. It emphasizes the diversity of experience and the validity of each person's experience. It seeks to develop an understanding of both the totality of oppression, and its specific manifestations, as the precondition for developing an anti-discriminatory practice relevant to all spheres of social work (Langan, 1992b). Over the past decade elements of the radical critique, of feminist, anti-racist and anti-discriminatory social work, have been increasingly absorbed into mainstream social work. For example, CCETSW, the body that supervises social work training, has adopted a commitment to a detailed code of anti-discriminatory practice. All social work courses are now obliged to teach students from an anti-discriminatory perspective and an awareness of these issues is expected of every qualifying social worker (CCETSW, 1991).

The significance of the adoption of the anti-discriminatory agenda by the social work establishment remains controversial. Some regard this as the successful achievement of at least some of the goals of the radical movement of the 1970s. Others are more sceptical, fearing that the old radicals have been incorporated and their principles compromised. In his survey of radical social work, Simpkin noted the irony that 'much of the radical rhetoric which remains is at present experienced as being imposed from above, whether by progressive Labour councils or by senior managers' (Simpkin, 1989, p. 160). As autonomous women's and anti-racist movements lost momentum in the generally hostile climate of the 1980s, former activists looked to government agencies, established professional bodies, local councils, even social services managers to take the lead in implementing aspects of the equal opportunities agenda.

Thus, for example, an official report published in 1991 by the Department of Health Social Services Inspectorate, entitled *Women in Social Services: a Neglected Resource*, proposed a wide range of positive actions to make social services departments more attractive and accessible to women employees (DHSSI, 1991). The report was imbued with the feminist principles of the seventies, from equal opportunities policies to measures for 'changing attitudes and behaviour' in relation to problems such as organizational culture and sexual harassment. While it acknowledged the contributions of well-known feminists (and some male leftwingers), it included a foreword by the Conservative health minister Virginia Bottomley.

Anti-racist activists too are inclined to look towards state agencies, or even to the new mixed economy of welfare, to push forward the anti-racist agenda. Connelly notes that the ascendancy of market forces and managerialism in social services means that the commitment of council politicians and senior managers to anti-racist policies is 'now even more important than...in the past' to the advance of multi-racialism (Connelly, 1990, p. 74). She urges 'individual black managers or local black groups' to seize the opportunities offered by the new mixed economy of welfare, advising them to 'ensure that they are equipped to bid for sites hived off by the department, or to enter the competitive tendering process' (Connelly, 1990, p. 75).

Elements of the radical critique have also been absorbed by social work's leading professional body, the British Association of Social Workers, one target of *CaseCon* in the 1970s. Its code of ethics has been modified, according to Bamford, 'to reflect the increased emphasis on clear statements against racism and discrimination on grounds of sexual orientation' (Bamford, 1990, p. 46). Thus anti-discriminatory principles have been assimilated into the professional identity of social work as part of the rearguard defence conducted by BASW against the relentless stream of attacks on the profession:

> The new professionalism has been much influenced...by the more committed social action stance of radical social workers. The legitimacy of social change as a preoccupation of social workers to stand alongside individual work has been codified in the ethical prescriptions of professional associations. Race and gender issues are being incorporated into discussions about ethics as the profession takes a wider view of its social values.
>
> (Bamford, 1990, p. 60).

Although Bamford welcomes these developments, he may underestimate the problem that, by adopting a more culturally relativist view, social work's claim to a coherent and unified professional knowledge-base, and its claims to professional status, are inevitably undermined. Simpkin's more sober conclusion is that 'while radical practice has in some ways become more integrated, radicalism itself has become diluted' (pp. 171–2).

4   FUTURE TRENDS

> Changes in political economy in tandem with attendant ideological shifts during the 1970s and 1980s have created a new welfare consensus in which the 'ambiguous' profession of social work has become subjected to greater public critique. Public criticism has in turn fuelled the willingness of certain aspects of the media to adopt an increasingly hostile posture towards social work and thereby complete a vicious circle.
>
> (Franklin and Parton, 1991, p. 48)

Franklin and Parton further argue that 'social workers have become a symbol for the public sector', and that 'media representations of social workers articulate a broader antipathy to the social democratic state as a provider of goods and services'. It does indeed appear that social workers have borne the brunt of popular abuse of the welfare state and that the social services departments are in the front line of attempts to restructure the role of the state in the mixed economy of welfare in the 1990s.

But what are the elements of the 'new welfare consensus' that are likely to shape the development of personal social services in coming years? There is no doubt that after two decades there is now little confidence in the capacity of social work to change the world for the better, or even to enhance life for more than a small number of individuals.

> It is hard now to remember the sense of optimism, the belief in the capacity of social workers to make a real impact on the lives of the vulnerable, disadvantaged and disturbed that characterized the time between the publication of the Seebohm report and the advent of the social services department.
>
> (Bamford, 1990, p. ix).

Much more pragmatic, even cynical, perspectives now prevail. For Webb and Wistow, social services staff are 'the night toil workers — or the social hygienists — of the twentieth century'; they are 'asked to cope with and conceal the unacceptable problems, tensions and social disasters of a complex society undergoing long-term, relative decline' (Webb and Wistow, 1987, p. 212). Far from the Seebohm conception of a comprehensive, preventive, rehabilitative approach to social problems, social workers are now reduced to offering a service of last resort in an overall climate of uncertainty and disillusionment.

Groups representing oppressed sections of society who once looked to social work for redress have come to a more sober assessment of its capacities. They are now inclined to turn in disappointment elsewhere: 'the contribution which social services can make to achieving social change may become over-valued; social services are in fact relatively marginal and powerless when compared to other social institutions' (Roys, 1988, p. 231).

A sense of reduced horizons and lowered expectations now prevails in public attitudes towards the personal social services. Although we devoted more or less equal space to considering 'challenges from above' and 'challenges from the margins', there can be no doubt that these challenges have had a differential impact. The pressures from the Government and the Treasury, from local authority administrators, the courts, the police and the mass media have proved much more influential in shaping the structure and practice of social services than the demands of client groups, anti-discriminatory movements and radical social workers.

While such challenges have undoubtedly had an impact on the ethics, theory and practice of social work, that practice has itself been increasingly circumscribed and reshaped by the financial, organizational and legislative changes of the 1980s and 1990s. Social work has become more tightly framed between the new 'mixed economy of care' on the one hand and the imposition of greater statutory and legal controls on the other. In some ways, these new constraints even embody aspects of the 'challenges from the margins', but they do so selectively and rarely on the terms established by those challenges. So, although they may represent checks on the powers of social work, they do not involve any transfer of power to service users directly. Rather, they create either legal or purchasing 'proxies' whose role it is to represent users' interests.

The dominant trends in social work are moves away from the professional and political optimism embodied in the Seebohm Report. It is no longer assumed that the state will support welfare needs: they must now be sought in the mixed economy. It is no longer assumed that the ambition of social work is to provide universal services — a door on which anyone might knock. Rather, services must be 'targeted' on those in danger or in need. It is no longer assumed that social work is almost a profession, able to understand and respond to the gamut of human misery. Rather, social work's claims to professional expertise lie in ruins. The 'social work task' is increasingly fragmented, not merely in relation to different client groups, but into the functions of assessment, supervision, purchasing, management and care servicing.

The generic social worker is already obsolete. Although the social work title may have survived it now covers a wide variety of activities. A minority of social services workers are being transformed into managers and specialist workers in the spheres of child protection and mental health. The countervailing trend is towards the deskilling of caring functions, by devolving them to poorly trained (and poorly paid) care workers, or to the voluntary or informal sectors. Even the elite social workers are obliged to work under the close supervision of the courts and within tight, if devolved, budgets. Social work faces a troubled and uncertain future.

REFERENCES

Baldock, J. (1989) 'United Kingdom — a perpetual crisis of marginality' in Munday, B. (ed.) *The Crisis in Welfare: an International Perspective on Social Services and Social Work*, Hemel Hempstead, Harvester Wheatsheaf, pp. 23–50.

Ball, W., Gulam, W. and Troyna, B. (1990) 'Pragmatism or retreat? Funding policy, local government and the marginalization of anti-racist education' in Ball, W. and Solomons, J. (eds).

Ball, W. and Solomons, J. (eds) (1990) *Race and Local Politics,* London, Macmillan.

Ball, W. and Solomons, J. (1990) 'Racial equality and local politics' in Ball, W. and Solomons, J. (eds) pp. 3–21.

Bamford, T. (1990) *The Future of Social Work*, London, Macmillan Education Ltd.

Barclay, P. (1982) *Social Workers: Their Role and Tasks*, London, National Institute for Social Work, Bedford Square Press.

Bolger, S., Corrigan, P., Docking, J., and Frost, N. (1981) *Towards Socialist Welfare Work*, London, Macmillan.

Brewer, C. and Lait, J. (1980) *Can Social Work Survive?* London, Temple Smith.

Brook, E. and Davis, A. (eds) (1985) *Women, the Family and Social Work*, London, Tavistock.

Brown, P., Hadley, R. and White, K. J. (1982) 'A case for neighbourhood-based social work and social services' in Barclay, P. pp. 219–35.

Butler-Sloss, E. (1988) *Report of the Inquiry into Child Abuse in Cleveland 1987*, presented to the Secretary of State for Social Services by the Right Honourable Lord Butler-Sloss DBE, London, HMSO.

Clarke, J. and Newman, J. (1993) 'Managing to survive? Dilemmas of changing organisational forms in the public sector' in Deakin, N. and Page, R. (eds) *The Costs of Welfare*, Social Policy Association/Avebury.

Clarke, J., Langan, M. and Lee, P. (1980) 'Social work: the conditions of crisis', in Carlen, P. and Collison, M. (eds) *Radical Issues in Criminology*, Oxford, Martin Robertson, pp. 178–95.

CCETSW (1991) *Rules and Requirements for the Diploma in Social Work*, London, CCETSW (Second Edition).

Cohen, S. (1985) *Visions of Social Control: Crime, Punishment and Classification*, Cambridge, Polity Press.

Connelly, N. (1990) 'Social services departments: the process and progress of change' in Ball, W. and Solomons, J. (eds) pp. 62–77.

Corrigan, P. and Leonard, P. (1978) *Social Work Practice Under Capitalism: a Marxist Approach*, London, Macmillan.

DHSS (1985) *Review of Child Care Law*, London, HMSO.

DHSSI (Department of Health Social Services Inspectorate) (1991) *Women in Social Services: a Neglected Resource*, London, HMSO.

Dominelli, L. and McLeod, E. (1989) *Feminist Social Work*, London, Macmillan.

Flynn, N. (1987) 'Delegating financial responsibility and policy making in social services departments', *Public Money*, March.

Franklin, B. and Parton, N. (eds), (1991) *Social Work, the Media and Public Relations,* London, Routledge.

Gordon, P. (1990) 'A dirty war: the new right and local authority anti-racism' in Ball, W. and Solomons, J. (eds).

Hallet, C. (ed.) (1989) *Women and Social Service Departments*, Hemel Hempstead, Harvester Wheatsheaf.

Hanmer, J. and Statham, D. (1988) *Women and Social Work: Towards a Woman-Centred Practice*, London, Macmillan.

Hughes, R. D. and Bhaduri, R. (1987) *Social Services for Ethnic Minorities and Race and Culture in Social Service Delivery*, Manchester, DHSS Social Services Inspectorate NW Region.

Jones, C. (1983) *State Social Work and the Working Class*, London, Macmillan.

Jones, K. (1988) *Experience in Mental Health: Community Care and Social Policy*, London, Sage.

Langan, M. and Day, L. (1992) *Women, Oppression and Social Work*, London, Routledge.

Langan, M. and Lee, P. (1989) 'Whatever happened to radical social work?' in Langan, M. and Lee, P. (eds) *Radical Social Work Today*, London, Unwin Hyman, pp. 1–18.

Langan, M. (1990) 'Community care in the 1990s', *Critical Social Policy*, 29, Autumn, pp. 58–70.

Langan, M. (1992a) 'Who cares?: women in the mixed economy of welfare' in Langan, M and Day, L. (eds).

Langan, M. (1992b) 'Women and social work in the 1990s' in Langan, M. and Day, L. (eds).

McCarthy, M. (1989) 'Personal social services' in McCarthy, M. (ed.) *The New Politics of Welfare: an Agenda for the 1990s?* London, Macmillan.

Marchant, H. and Wearing, B. (eds) (1986) *Gender Reclaimed: Women in Social Work*, Sydney, Hale and Iremonger.

NALGO, (1989) *Social Work in Crisis: a Study of Conditions in Six Local Authorities*, London, NALGO.

Parton, N. (1991) *Governing the Family: Child Care, Child Protection and the State*, London, Macmillan.

Pinker, R.A. (1982) 'An alternative view' in Barclay, P. pp. 236–62.

Rooney, B. (1987) *Racism and Resistance to Change: a Study of the Black Social Workers' Project, Liverpool Social Services Department 1975–1985*, Liverpool, Department of Sociology, University of Liverpool.

Rooney, B. (1982) 'Black social workers in white departments' in Cheetham J. (ed.) *Social Work and Ethnicity*, London, NISW/George Allen and Unwin, pp. 184–96.

Roys, P. (1988) 'Social services' in Bhat, A. Carr-Hill, R. and Ohri, S. (eds) *Britain's Black Population: a New Perspective* (Second edition), London, Gower, pp. 208–36.

Simpkin, M. (1989) 'Radical social work: lessons for the 1990s' in Carter, P., Jeffs, T. and Smith, M. (eds) *Social Work and Social Welfare: Year Book 1*, Milton Keynes, Open University Press, pp. 159–74.

Smith, D. (1983) *From Seebohm to Barclay: the Changing Political Nature of the Organization of Social Work*, Discussion paper, Department of Social Administration, University of Manchester.

Social Services Committee (1984) *Children in Care* (HC 360), London, HMSO.

Solomons, J. and Ball, W. (1990) 'New initiatives and the possibilities of reform' in Ball, W. and Solomons, J. (eds), pp. 210–24.

Webb, A. and Wistow, G. (1987), *Social Work, Social Care and Social Planning: the Personal Social Services Since Seebohm*, London, Longman.

Young, K. (1990) 'Approaches to policy development in the field of equal opportunities' in Ball, W. and Solomons, J. (eds) pp. 22–42.

STUDY QUESTIONS

1   What are the implications of recent legislation for the organization of social work?

2   What are the implications of the move to a 'mixed economy' of care for social work's relationship to 'diversity'?

3   To what extent does social work's adoption of a commitment to 'anti-discriminatory' practice meet the challenges 'from the margins'?

4   Why has social work been the focus of such extensive public and political hostility?

5   To what extent, and in what ways, have challenges from the centre been more influential than challenges from the margins in shaping the future of social work?

INDEX